In the Name of the Father the Revolution Will Be Televised

Endurance

BY

A. ADISA BRECKENRIDGE-AYERS

DORRANCE PUBLISHING CO., INC.
PITTSBURGH, PENNSYLVANIA 15222

The opinions expressed herein are those of the author, who assumes complete and sole responsibility for them, and do not necessarily represent the views of the publisher or its agents.

For more information or to order additional books, please contact:
Dorrance Publishing Co., Inc.
701 Smithfield Street
Third Floor
Pittsburgh, Pennsylvania 15222
U.S.A.
1-800-788-7654
www.dorrancebookstore.com

DEDICATION

To my mother and the late Mrs. Black. My lovely mother, Dorothy Ayers-Breckenridge, insisted I attend church every Sunday. Without her commitment and conviction in Christ, which she instilled in me, I don't think I would have beaten the odds of life's many trials and tribulations of my past. To the late Mrs. Rachel Black, who always directed the choir and played the piano every Sunday morning. To the best of sisterhood!

CONTENTS

Preface

"Those who do not learn from history are doomed to repeat it." The same problems that plagued ancient Rome and caused its destruction are starting to occur in our country. If we do not stop the negative output and negative nonchalant attitude towards global warming and addictive dependence on foreign oil, we will destroy ourselves, even if we are the greatest, most powerful nation in the world today.

Acknowledgment

To Beverly Kerr, my best friend and real true-life angel. Where would I be without you my friend? To Lisa Sanders, George and Marie Samudio, whose friendships walked in while the rest of the world walked out. And to those who believed in me, especially those in my extended family whose thoughts and prayers comforted me during my trials and tribulations. Special thanks to Santiago Banchon for his angel-heart and his unselfish commitment to our friendship which will always persevere. His wisdom and knowledge will always be cherished for making my dream a reality.

ACKNOWLEDGMENT 11

"We must forever conduct our struggle on the high plain of dignity and discipline. We must not allow our creative protest to degenerate into physical violence. We must rise to the majestic heights of meeting physical force with soul force."

—Reverend Martin Luther King, Jr.

"The belief that God will do everything for man is as untenable as the belief that man can do everything for himself. It too, is based on a lack of faith. We must learn that to expect God to do everything while we do nothing is not faith, but superstition."—Reverend Martin Luther King, Jr.

Special thanks to Kay Midro for her word processing skills. Her commitment and patience in working with me on this project over the years will always be most appreciated.

Special thanks to S. Evan Walters, publisher, Abel Creative Services, for an honest critique of the manuscript during its final draft and encouraging me to tell my story.

The following sections were reprinted by permission from *The Urantia Book*, published by the Urantia Foundation, Chicago, Illinois: "The Truth About Religion," "The Truth About Prayer," "The Evolution of Prayer," "Conditions of Effective Prayer," "The Truth About Sin."

This message contains a revolutionary agenda for all men, women, and children who serve under ONE CREATOR for all mankind.

Divine love,
Adisa

Introduction

Ronnie Was a Good Man

My name is Tyrone William Breckenridge. Even though this was my given name at birth, my mother's family and friends always referred to me as "Ronnie" when I was growing up. As I matured and began to understand about racism and culture in the historical context, I made the decision to legally change my name, as an attribute to my heritage, to Adisa Breckenridge-Ayers. Adisa is Afrikan which means one who makes his meaning clear. Breckenridge was my father's sir name, and Ayers is my mother's maiden name. All of these names have significant influence in my life and have given me the strength to endure the many trials and tribulations and to continue the struggle for equality and justice for everyone.

I was raised in the church, the Afrikan Methodist Episcopal Church. I am currently a member and therefore, I accept and pursue the responsibilities that embody the sacred tradition that encourages Afrikan American people to learn about their rightful and spiritual place in the world. I was inspired to write because if I screamed and hollered, nobody would take me seriously.

The inception of this spirit to write and evoke my emotions was attributable in part to my unfair and untimely incarceration along with the prejudices and insensitivity of law enforcement ("A Rush to Judgement"). American justice is rested upon having lots of money and who you are connected to. American justice should be called "just-us", those of us who are privileged and rich. "Just-us" has humiliated and embarrassed me in their "Rush to Judgement", "just-us" maliciously set out to destroy my credibility, economically and socially. My sincere empathy for women who have been raped (literally as well as figuratively) is exemplified when compared to

America's unjust criminal justice system. I was physically and emotionally violated, penetrated and displayed naked before the world denying me the opportunity to make bail, with no one able to come to my aid to rescue me from this relentless attack that occurred at four o'clock in the afternoon on December 19, 1993.

As I look back, better is the victorious one who has control over the pen as opposed to the one who yields with the sword. It was Jesus who said, "To live by it, is to die by it." I, Ronnie Be Good, am a living testimony and a witness to that simple, yet most powerful parable.

At 9 years old, I remember feeling totally bored, alienated from the rest of the third grade class, talking with one of my classmates, discussing how wonderful it would be to become a real bonafide "blood brother." My classmate hastily agreed, since we didn't get much attention and recognition in class, we were obligated to amuse ourselves. Much to my surprise, my friend pulled this little pocket-knife out of his pocket and said, "let's do it!" I did it and my friend went chicken. This was my first public act of rebellion. My classmate cut me on my hand between my index finger and thumb. I bled profusely until my teacher took notice and nervously shuffled me off to the nurse's station. I survived, but I still have the scar to remind me of this foolish ordeal.

I came from a family of eight, growing up next to the oldest of four brothers and one sister. Real or not, I constantly felt the need to provide and protect. Providing was equated with stealing and protecting meant fighting and establishing a bad-boy mentality. I justified the need to provide by falsely blaming my father, because my dad sometimes had the tendency to blow a lot of extra money at the track. There seemed many a time we were economically stressed because there was never enough money around to constantly feed, clothe, and pay rent and utility bills for a family of eight.

Consequently, I thought the best thing to do was take control with my bad-boy mentality and convince and organize my younger brothers into a semi-professional thieving ring, targeting the local "ACME" grocery store, except for "baby boy," my youngest brother Darryl, who just happened to turn out to be the Chief of Police in the small middle class town I grew up in. He was always against crime and it certainly paid off for him. My other brothers are quite successful too. My brother, Terry, is a certified High Pressure Boiler Operator and Senior Maintenance mechanic who currently works for the Monmouth County Correctional Institute. My brother, Bill, is in civil service, working at Fort Knox, KY. He was a TV cameraman for Fort Knox TV. He has thirty years service and is still currently working at Fort Knox. My brother, Kevin, has worked as a U.S. postal worker for almost thirty years and my only sister, Crystal, is an evangelist and a missionary.

Stealing from the local grocery store was especially easy during the winter months when it was cold. We had long winter coats, which we took the seams out of the pockets so we could drop as much food into the lining as possible without being conspicuous. These were the good ole days, before they had "floor-walkers" and cameras.

Believe it or not, we did this successfully for about three years. We even had our friends join us on occasion to ransack the grocery store and then come back to our house and have a great big fiesta. The only reason we stopped was because the "ACME" started hiring "floor-walkers" who made it more difficult and someone also snitched and mom found out and mentioned it to dad who whipped all of our asses. But, from that day forward, there always seemed to be more food in the house and mom became the official finance director.

Mom always seemed to be in charge of all major decisions. Pop always worked every day starting at four a.m. to about noon; he was a trash collector for the city of Fair Haven, N.J. After work, he would go to the track and bet on the horses. He also worked on farms in the area and took care of the stables. Pop just seemed to be the one who seldom spoke with empathy, but always carried the grim look of life's toll across his face. If he got mad or was instructed by mom to punish you, he would pick up anything in sight and beat you, belts, hangers, sticks, etc. There was no such thing as child abuse in those days.

Mom was always religious and sent us to Sunday school and church every Sunday. The main rule was if you didn't go to church on Sunday, then you couldn't go out and play on Sunday. Being that I had four younger brothers and the fact that we played football every Sunday, the rest of the neighborhood kids depended on us to make up most of the team. It was unthinkable not to be able to play on Sunday. Thank God this was always the case because I do believe church is where I gained the most stability in terms of learning basic ethics and morals, that somehow guided me through to sustain and continue to overcome life's trials and tribulations.

For the next few years, school and home were the main focal point in my life. Problems in school escalated. I lost interest in school and being the only black in the classroom, at this point I tried to seek attention by being labeled a "troublemaker." I was kicked out of school on a regular basis – for reasons of truancy, stealing, fighting and verbal abuse. At this juncture, my mother thought she could better discipline me and have more control over me if she were to take employment with the local police department. She was hired as a school crossing guard. As I reflect back, I do understand her logic of where her mind set was. It was comforting for her, but extremely miserable for me because I became a target and convenience for teachers who had the permission and liberty of snatching me up, (literally), and taking me out to my mother across the street to my mother's "station" every time I acted up. I would sit in her car until it was time to go home. I would rebel even after I got home, got beaten and promised to be a good kid. This scenario lasted for approximately four years until I was transferred to the intermediate school. There I had my freedom, nobody was watching over me. I guess with this newfound freedom and having to walk over a half mile to school, helped me to become occupied with new adventures. I managed to stay out of trouble for the most part, for two consecutive years.

After finishing at the intermediate level, I was transferred to junior high school. Unfortunately, it was located at the same school where I had previous trouble and I was once again at the whim of the teachers, because my mom worked at this school and everyone knew who she was.

Seventh grade was not as horrible as I imagined it to be. I loved science and my science teacher. He was a gentleman who really cared about his students. I managed to stay out of trouble for an entire year. However, the eighth grade proved disastrous. I found myself being neglected and seeking devious attention by disrespecting authority and getting into fights.

I never forgot the day I got into a fight on the playground and was immediately taken to mom, who was on duty right out in front of the school. This teacher grabs me by my "pompadour" from the midst of the fight and drags me all the way from the playground to my mother's car. I got a backhand and was threatened with bodily harm that would be served later by my dad once I got home. I had such a bad year and my grades were so poor, they wouldn't even allow me to participate in graduation. I know the only reason they sent me on to high school, was the fact they had a chance to get rid of me and it would have broken my mother's heart if I didn't make it to high school.

My high school days didn't last very long. In fact, I managed to stay in school for only four months before I was permanently expelled. Mom and dad were furious to say the least. Both parents were employed by the town, and I was now the "talk of the town" and it wasn't a good thing, especially in a very small town of fifteen hundred or less. Everyone knew everyone else's business and this is where the original phrase "It takes a village to raise a child" originated. I was sixteen, out of school, and had no job. Mom, and especially dad, couldn't tolerate me staying home doing absolutely nothing, so I found an alternative school to hang out for a while with different folks and negative influences. This was fun and this is when I got a chance to work half days to make some money to buy weed and beer. Everything went fine for a while, but then, with these newfound friends, I got introduced to dealers who had plenty of weed, acid, heroin and most days would be spent at the beach instead of school. Eventually I quit and was idle, I began to sell marijuana and use heroin.

* * *

I turned seventeen on December 8, 1968. I remember it was on a Sunday and on Sunday, all black people went to the movie house. On that particular night, the original "Night of the Living Dead" was playing. Everyone seemed to be enjoying the movie until the end when the only black guy in the movie gets killed. There appeared to be an argument in the back of where I was sitting. You could hear people cursing, yelling and screaming at one of the ushers. Next thing I know, the place is flooded with police. Then suddenly, the police were hitting people with nightsticks. Things got totally out of control. People were fighting all over the place, all the way out into the street. (A total melee). I remember hitting the police who was beating someone with a stick and the next thing I remember is being kicked and punched by the police, getting handcuffed and being sent to jail. I was charged with assault on a police officer and starting a riot. My Mom and Dad had to come to jail. I was released to their custody until the trial.

Mother contacted a lawyer and the lawyer advised that I would probably go to "Jamesburg", a juvenile detention center and do at least two years in light of these charges and being out of school and having no job. He said the only option that might be available is that I join the military with their signed consent. I agreed, it seemed the lesser of two evils. Two weeks later I was on a train headed for Paris Island, South Carolina to join the United States Marine Corps.

My time in the marines turned out more disastrous than rewarding. Boot camp was awesome, I got in great physical shape, learned discipline, and how to protect myself, "once a marine, always a marine." Hoorah! Everything was going okay, a few bar fights because there was still lots of overt prejudice on base. I made private first class and had immediate orders to go to Vietnam, but fate had it that I get in a serious car accident and break my collarbone. They gave my orders to someone else, I got very discouraged and my attitude changed for the worse. I joined a Black Panther affiliate and my allegiance fell to the party instead of the Corps. I asked to be discharged on an undesirable discharge, they said no, and set me up with trumped up charges, since I already had a couple of article 32's. I had no real defense, I was determined to get out of the three year contract with the marines, so I made a plea agreement to get the whole ordeal over with as fast as I could. Something I will always look back at as extreme stupid pride. I received fifteen months confinement to hard labor at the Marine Corps/ Navy prison in Portsmouth, New Hampshire and a bad conduct discharge. I was discharged from the maximum-security prison in March 1971.

Now I was free to go back home to New Jersey. However, returning home after being kicked out of the marines with a bad conduct discharge and without a high school education was less than desirable, especially in terms of finding work without appropriate education and skills. So, the only way I knew how to make money was selling marijuana and move into the fast lane with the pimps, whores and drug dealers. I was easily accepted into this group. I was young, a fast talker, and could hold my own in the streets.

My career on the streets came to an abrupt halt one evening in September of 1972. I was arrested and charged with armed robbery. This was my first arrest as an adult so I thought I would get a light sentence, but to everyone's surprise, especially my mother, who I thought was about to faint, yell or scream as the judge passed the sentence. The judge gave me six to ten years in the state penitentiary.

The next four and one-half years would eventually change my whole life around. State prison would be the most horrible experience I would have encountered in my entire eighteen years on planet Earth. If anyone goes to prison "back in the old days" and say they weren't afraid is a liar and not in their right frame of mind. The prison was full of killers, perverts, thugs and child molesters. Back in the day, they still had "free-weights" and everybody looked like a page out of Greek mythology, "Atlas and Hercules." Back in the old days there was no "prison rights" and conditions were inhumane. There was no separation of fags and bad-men. It was survival based on your skill level and the will to live amongst the wretched and doomed.

I decided to use my time as productively as possible. I would work out on my body for about ten hours a day, lifting weights and doing calisthenics. The rest of the day was spent "learning", reading and writing anything and everything to make good use of my time. I signed up for college too. The first ever college program for inmates was offered by Mercer County Community College, Mercerville, New Jersey. Although I never completed my high school education, here was the opportunity to get an education. Maybe my fate would change someday. The education department was look-ing for volunteers to enter into the program. They did not do any serious checking for credentials, so I faked and forged a G.E.D. and had no problem enrolling in the two-year college program. During my enrollment, I made the Dean's list three times. I was the first inmate to graduate from college from inside the penitentiary. I received my Associates in Science, a two-year degree from a community college. I was proud, my entire family was proud. After four and one half years in prison, I was paroled. I successfully contin-ued my educational pursuits and obtained my Bachelors in Sociology and Masters in Education.

The next five years would consist of a broken marriage, plenty of drugs and alcohol. I moved from New Jersey to Silver Springs, Maryland. I land-ed my first job in Corrections. My marriage was a disaster! Thank God there were no children. I was certainly not ready to settle down, so I split town one night, leaving everything behind except important papers and returned to New Jersey.

Angry at myself, I continued to use drugs. Cocaine was new to me and I enjoyed the high. I used to mix coke with heroin and was completely addicted within six months.

I did manage to land another job with Corrections in New Jersey, but my habit became so intense and expensive I had to eventually hit the streets and hustle. A nine to five job was too slow and waiting two weeks for a paycheck seemed absurd. I connected with an old "G" from the penitentiary and started selling coke and heroin. I became a self-made enforcer, taking off other drug dealers and strong-arming potential clients. We would go to New York, some-times twice a day to pick up coke and heroin, come back to Jersey side, sell half the product and use the other half. At this point, I was back to old habits that would eventually lead me back to prison, if I didn't get a grip real soon!

My mom wondered how I would have money and no job. She sensed I was using and was totally out of control. Sleep all day and out all night (The Vampire Syndrome). I was in high survival mode taking off other junkies and dealers until first light. She told me one day that I had to leave. She said she would help me leave the area if I could take on a part-time job and stop doing drugs. I took her offer, quit cold turkey for five days, sweating, vomiting and going through hell until I was able to eat and get my strength back. My sister had just moved to Hawaii and that was my ticket out of New Jersey.

I relocated to Hawaii from the east coast in the fall of 1987 because I needed a time-out from alcohol, drugs and apathy. I was in the climax of self-destruction and I needed to pull out before I ejaculated into an abyss of no return. It was a rough road to accomplish what I had achieved and it would be suicide to continue down this immoral road of self-destruction. I vowed I would never ever return to prison and try to stay drug free.

When I arrived in Hawaii, the place I call "The Desire to Desire", I was in awe. Having de-planed, the hot air engulfed me enough to be distracted by the beautiful smell of the leis (flowers). Then having left the airport, I made a detour to the ocean. I was amazed at the sight of the blue majestic ocean, not green nor brown or filled with sewage. Henceforth, I naturally just fell in love with "mother nature" as it was connected to Hawaii. Hawaii, my home away from home, October, my favorite month in Hawaii; you can at least see a rainbow once or twice a day. Unfortunately, the Hawaiians like the Native American Indian and the Native American Black will never be completely emancipated from white modern-day colonialism because of generations of institutionalized racism that has been complacent over time.

Eventually, I would refrain from using, quitting is easy, it's been done a thousand times, but to quit is impossible, to refrain is attainable since substance abuse is an emotional and physical impairment.

I would continue to get off and on the wagon for many years until the divine spirit broke me. God works many wonders in a loving mysterious way. Addiction is a very serious, complex phenomenon. I believe the predisposition of an addiction is attributed to a combination of factors: hereditary, socially and mentally. I realized I have an addictive genetic trait.

Finding work in Hawaii was not difficult. I immediately was employed as a security person and an assistant special education teacher. Since then, I have been employed by the Department of Health and assigned to the Parole Board and Hawaii's Correctional Prison system. I also managed a group home for the mentally ill person(s).

I was basically very happy and content with my life. Nonetheless, all of this was to change on December 19, 1993. At approximately four o'clock in the afternoon, I was arrested. I became a suspect of a robbery at the motel I stayed at the previous evening. The motel had in fact gone on record as being robbed two weeks prior to my stay. This event was allegedly executed by a black man with a beard, thus beginning this unimaginable ordeal.

The absurdity of this whole affair would take on many ludicrous and absolutely incredible turns. Subsequently, at the time of my arrest, I was serving two terms of federal probation. On May 4, 1989, I was placed on five years of probation for being a felon in possession of a firearm and <u>not in commission of a new crime.</u> But because a felon is a person who is denied his constitutional rights of the Second Amendment for life: "The right of the people to keep and bear arms, shall not be infringed." The government thereby denies me the right to defend myself or my family with a legally purchased firearm.

The firearm was a gift for my father which I purchased in Radcliff, Kentucky, while I was visiting my brother. I inadvertently packaged the gun in my carry-on luggage. Upon my arrival at the check-in desk at the Cincinnati airport, I was told it was too late to put my luggage on the conveyor to be placed in the cargo department of the plane. Consequently, I was arrested for not declaring the weapon and released on bond the following day and took the next flight out to New Jersey.

I thought that this would be the end of that episode—but I was wrong! In March of 1989, while staying at my sister's house in Hawaii, I was arrested by the Alcohol, Tobacco and Firearm "Agent." I was charged with a felon in possession of a fire-arm (the incident at the Cincinnati airport). I was placed on a $10,000 signature bond and was extradited to Covington, Kentucky to make a plea. I pled guilty because I was unaware that I could plead nolo contendere (no contest) and I thought it would be moot to try and defend myself in that neck of the woods, "red-neck country." I should have stood my ground and fought for my right to bear arms regardless of the label of being called a felon. This law needs to be addressed and changed. All ex-convicts are not always criminals and they should have their constitutional rights restored to them after a ten-year waiting period. All we ask is a chance to prove our worth. To resolve the matter in Covington, Kentucky, I pleaded guilty and was placed on five years of probation. In the interim, I changed my guilty plea to nolo contendere and on February 25, 1991, I was placed on another additional three years of probation to run concurrent with the five years of probation; for falsifying the plea agreement of being a felon in possession of a firearm.

Over the preceding years, I had successfully adhered to the probation conditions and was about to be released from supervision. My five-year term of probation supervision was to expire on May 3, 1994, and my three-year term of supervision was to expire on February 24, 1994. Since I was arrested on December 19, 1993, as a robbery suspect and released pending further investigation, my federal probation officer saw fit to revoke my probation because of this arrest. He petitioned the federal court that I be detained with a <u>No-Bail</u>, because of my alleged conduct: "that on December 4, 1993, the subject (I) engaged in a law-violating activity, to wit, robbery, first degree, in violation of the general terms and conditions of my probation." A court order with a no-bail warrant was issued and on January 10, 1994, I was once again arrested and detained, this time by the United States Marshal, for my alleged conduct in the robbery of the motel and not much for the technical violations of failure to increase my fine payment and failure to tell my employer that I was on probation, that the government previously attempted to revoke my probation in November of 1993, and failed.

Ironically, on February 23, 1994, the day before I was to successfully complete my term of three years of federal supervision, the government moved to revoke my probation for the technical violations and sentenced me to six months of imprisonment for the original conduct of falsifying a federal document.

Then on April 28, 1994, I received a bench warrant from the State of Hawaii, indicting me for robbery in the first degree, for that of the motel I stayed at on December 18, 1993. Finally, on November 23, 1994, I was acquitted by the jury of the alledged robbery. However, during this entire interim I remained in custody by the federal government for this alledged conduct that I was absolved of. Astounding as it may sound, it doesn't end here. I wasn't able to walk out of the courtroom a free man like most people, because the federal government continued a "no-bail" detainer on me and subsequently placed me back into federal custody. This entire affair was becoming absurd, excruciating and very frustrating.

On December 12, 1994, I was revoked for my term of five years of federal supervision, which was imposed on May 4, 1989 and which was to expire on May 3, 1994. (Note: When I was detained by the federal government on January 10, 1994, the five-year term of probation stopped.) However, it was previously agreed upon by the U.S. government that they would not pursue this revocation if I was acquitted of the State charge of robbery. This proved not to be true! The government and my attorney agreed to resolve this dispute by having me admit to my previous technical violations once again, that I had already admitted to during the revocation of my three-year term of federal supervision. What happened to the principle of double jeopardy?

If I did not agree to this arrangement, the U.S. attorney would have prosecuted me for violations of federal laws, such as possession of a weapon as a felon or extortion pursuant to the Hobbs Act, arising from the alleged robbery conduct on December 19, 1993 of which I was acquitted of on November 23, 1994.

Upon accepting this agreement (with little or no choice of reprisal) the government moved to revoke my five-year term of probation and sentenced me to 12 months of prison to run consecutively to the six months of imprisonment I received on February 23, 1994. I was sentenced on December 12, 1994 and released from prison on May 3, 1995. I did not commit any crime.

However, as a result of this madness to save my life, I became angry, bitter and disappointed with the criminal justice system. This mockery of an inept judicial system had willfully and deliberately slandered my good name.

I became a victim of "the war against crime." I spent 16 months in prison because I am a proud black man and because I am an ex-felon.

It is said, "Once you commit a crime, you pay the price for the rest of your natural born life." They are absolutely correct. I am living testimony to that fact. I naively thought that once I successfully got off parole, earned three separate college degrees, voted for three presidents, remained active in community affairs, and obeyed the law for the past thirteen years since my release from state prison, that I had paid my debt to society. "Wrong again." I was still an ex-convict, legally known as a felon. You are *never* allowed to forget it. Some twenty-five years later, I'm still wearing the lifelong badge of an ex-convict. Somewhere along the way I was tricked into believing this notion that rehabilitation was an attainable goal. I sincerely believed the concept of rehabilitation. How naïve I was. The rehabilitation concept is only as good as the paper it is written on. (Programs on paper). The criminal justice system does not want the ex-convict to become rehabilitated and successful. This would put a damper on the influx of money needed to support the big business machinery of Corrections, "bodies account for money." California's biggest employer is the Department of Corrections and the Sheriff Deputy's Division, not to mention the B.O.P. (Bureau of Prisons). This big business accounts for seven out of ten people released from prison who are eventually re-incarcerated not because they commit another crime, but because seventy percent of ex-convicts cannot get out of the vicious cycle of being branded. They are inevitably trapped from the beginning by being placed on parole, probation or supervised release—a watchdog system that encourages dependence, not *independence.*

It costs $1,734.00 a month to incarcerate a federal inmate and $56.00 a day to incarcerate a state inmate. (Number based on California prisons, other states may vary.) Over seventy-five percent of inmates in federal prison are in for drug offenses such as conspiracy for trafficking, possession and distribution. None of these crimes are against property or persons. These offenders do not need to be incarcerated with the few who need to be punished, they need alternative programs that address drug abuse and employment. The habitual recidivist, the career criminal, murderers, child molesters and rapists need to be confined. They are a menace to society. This does not mean to say they don't need treatment. On the contrary, they need psychiatric as well as social skills training before they can be released. They need to be gradually placed into community halfway houses, for at least twelve months to see if they are able to be trusted and also to see if they are acceptable and appropriate for treatment. After-care programming is a very vital component for inmates being released back into the community. These prior offenders should be tracked by sensitive and street-wise technicians, to help assist them in their transition and re-integration. If an ex-convict is successful and has properly maintained and avoided any further criminal activity for ten years, he should be eligible for a governor's pardon, nationally recognized. We need to start giving tangible acts of accomplishments for ex-offenders being an asset to their families and communities and who are drug free and crime free.

I defend this argument by illustrating the dynamics of my own personal experience as follows: I was crime free for thirteen years. Did I get a pardon for good behavior? No! Of course not. The state where I did the crime when I was nineteen years old has a no pardon policy for common ordinary people, unless of course you have political influence or connections with organized crime. This is also true when requesting a federal pardon. I had no influences or money, so consequently, I was denied a pardon. Hence, for the rest of my life, even though I have not lived in the state of New Jersey for any substantial amount of time, where this offense took place, I will always wear this badge of shame, "Put me down," labeled for life as an ex-felon, a commodity for my consumers, that being the judges, courts, lawyers, police, jails, and prisons across America. A product to be used and abused for the rest of my natural life. Perchance, maybe I will hide now that I am released from prison, become so low keyed and maintain just enough breathing room to hear pin drops, hoping not to stir trouble, trying to survive, hoping and praying that someone will hire me and give me a chance to live a normal life.

The trial for the robbery charge began on November 20, 1994. The only evidence the prosecutor had was the videotape of me which was taken during my stay at the motel on December 18, 1994, during check out time at twelve noon. There was no factual, material or circumstantial "crime scene" evidence brought into court. However, I was positively identified by the victim because I was a black man who wore a beard. I fit the description of the alleged robber, and that was sufficient enough reason to charge me with robbery. *"A black man who wore a beard."*

I was now facing twenty years for robbery. Also, another ten years from the federal government for probation violations. If convicted, the time would run consecutive not concurrent. I would have to spend at least thirty years in prison and be seventy-three years old if I had maxed out, meaning no parole.

Thank God this never happened. I was saved by His loving grace through perseverance and faith. Today, I do pray for all those innocent people who are still being persecuted and legally framed because of an inept criminal justice system and over-burdened public defender's office. I pray for all those brothers and sisters for spiritual uplifting and ask God to give them the strength to be strong in the hope that one day they will gain their freedom from their oppressors, if in fact they are innocent victims of the get tough crime policy. (Mandatory Drug Sentencing Laws).

Having clearly stated that which is true and accurate in my introduction, I am unequivocally aware of my past transgressions and dubious or lack of good judgment. Nonetheless, I have paid and re-paid my debt to society. I have been systematically and categorically let down by the same standards and values I have supported the majority of my adult life. But who am I to judge, I am no angel. Only a servant of my God, the Lord being my shepherd. I do not fear those who can kill my body and take my freedom. For they cannot and will not take away my faith. I say to you, "Believe in yourself and believe in your visions." The resurrection will come and liberate those who believe. The time is now, seize the opportunity and deliver yourself from this evil world. I finally achieved victory over my self-committed, self-destructiveness in the fall of 2000. This realization came after six years of playing and sucking the devils dick (smoking crystal methamphetamine), climaxed into the stabbing of a person in self-defense, hence getting arrested and almost being charged with attempted murder. Thank God, angels were dispatched and I was lifted out from the deep sin within the beautiful islands of Oahu and sent to the rolling hills of the Bluegrass state. Once again, saved by His grace!!!

I now know I have an addictive personality, so every day is a test. I believe in God because I realize I can't do it all by myself. I continue to work with troubled youth, the field in which I will have the most impact. That field is counseling youths who might be headed down the same road in life as I once did. I have worked at various Job Corps and will continue to do so until I retire. Today's youth are very fragile and extremely challenging.

Sincerely,
Ronnie Be Good

Genocide or Menticide

Genocide—it is apparent that the major research held both in open and in secret is involved today with issues that are genocidal in nature, some deliberately, others being unintentional, e.g. chemical warfare, gene therapy, cloning, population control (abortion used as a contraceptive), the decimation of the mainstream of our communities by H.I.V. and other deadly viruses, and the continued influx of illicit drugs into our communities.

DRUG AND ALCOHOL ABUSE

Smoking is more prevalent among Afrikan Americans than among Caucasians. Afrikan Americans have higher death rates from smoking-related diseases.

For example, 86 percent of deaths from lung cancer are attributed to smoking, and Afrikan American death rates for this ailment are more than twice that of Caucasians.

Alcohol abuse and addiction have created a myriad of problems among Afrikan Americans, Hispanics, Native Americans, Asians, and Eskimos. Alcohol abuse is the number one health problem among Afrikan Americans. Alcohol and drug abuse are both the cause and result of a plethora of other problems, including unemployment, crime, broken marriages, and debilitating physical disease. It is therefore no wonder there are so many dysfunctional families among minorities.

The current cocaine and "crack" epidemic among young Afrikan American males in inner cities is a clear example of environmental, cultural, economical, and generational disparity in the prevalence of chemical dependency and crime specific to these populations.

Environmental, economical, and familial factors actively reinforce and synergize the incidence of minority group chemical dependency among Afrikan American, Hispanic, Native American, Polynesians, and Asian youths. It is reasonable to assume that approximately 25 percent of these populations will manifest both syndromes.

Drug policy in America has historically been formed by racist notions. The first anti-drug laws were passed in California in the nineteenth century in response to exaggerated fears about opium use among immigrant Chinese workers. Cocaine laws were developed earlier this century to combat fears about Afrikan American men becoming crazed by the drug and raping white women. The first anti-marijuana legislation in the 1930s was aimed at similar myths about Mexican men.

Despite the racist origins of our drug laws, government reports on illegal drug use among different races in America reveal that a full 75 percent of all current illegal drug users in this country are white. Of the remaining 25 percent of Americans who use illegal drugs, only about 17 percent are black. Yet Afrikan Americans make up a full 45 percent of all Americans arrested in this country for drug use. This huge discrepancy certainly suggests racism in our justice system, though some argue that the poverty of many Afrikan Americans is equally responsible. Unlike middle-class white users, poor blacks who use drugs do not have the luxury of buying or using their drugs in private. Poverty forces them to commit their crimes in neighborhoods with a large police presence, making them particularly vulnerable to arrest. What is absolutely clear is that Afrikan Americans suffer disproportionately from the drug war. Whether racism is the cause of this discrepancy is less important than the actual impact of our current drug war: de facto racial discrimination against Afrikan Americans and other minorities.

AIDS Alert

To add fuel to the fire, the AIDS virus is now the leading killer of young to middle-aged Afrikan American adults. These findings were contained in a recent report by the National Center for Disease Control. According to this report, "between 1989 and 1991, H.I.V. infection was the number-one killer of Afrikan American adults from twenty-five to forty-four years of age." For Afrikan American men, that death rate is more than three times as high as their Caucasian counterparts. Equally alarming, H.I.V. infection was the leading cause of death in five of thirty states. H.I.V. infection was the leading cause of death for young Afrikan American men in twenty-six of eighty-one cities, including Portsmouth Virginia, and Elizabeth New Jersey. Among Afrikan American women, H.I.V. infection was the leading cause of death in ten of forty-nine cities, including Atlanta, Georgia, and Patterson, New Jersey.

CRIME AND PUNISHMENT

Some facts on the criminal justice system and people of color:

— More than 35 percent of black males between twenty and twenty-nine years old are in prison, on parole, or on probation.

— 700,00 Blacks are in prison systems; 430,000 are in college. If trends continue, by the year 2009, six of ten blacks will be in jail, addicted, or dead before age twenty-five.

— 90 percent of offenders sentenced to state and federal prisons for drug offenses were black or Latino.

— 70 percent of prison drug treatment slots went to whites in New York State in 1992.

— The percentage of increase in U.S. incarceration rates for white women between 1985 and 1995 in the U.S. was 143 percent; for black women the rate of increase was 204 percent—both due to the drug war.

— Percentage of people sentenced for crack offenses who were white and black respectively: 4.1 percent, 88 percent. Penalty in federal court for five grams of powder cocaine is one year maximum; for five grams of crack, five years minimum.

In Hawaii, incarceration rates for disadvantaged ethnic groups like Native Hawaiians and Samoans are very high in relation to their numbers in the population; some estimate that they make up 73 percent of the prison population.

Still more shocking are the alarming numbers of Afrikan Americans incarcerated. A report published September 13, 1994, by the Associated Press stated, "The United States has a higher rate of incarceration than any country in the world except Russia, according to a study released this year by a private group.

"The Sentencing Project, which promotes alternative sentencing, concluded that get-tough policies of the last two decades have failed to reduce violent crime. The study found there were 1.3 million inmates in American prisons, and the incarceration rate has reached an all-time high of 519 per 100,000 population, up 22 percent since 1989 The report found that Afrikan Americans are incarcerated at six times the rate of Caucasians, and that the 583,000 Afrikan American men in jails surpassed the 537,000 enrolled in higher education." Today there are 7.2 million inmates in jails and prisons across America. I wonder how many are Afrikan American?

Crime has become the number-one American tragedy because of the lack of a moral and ethical base which has manifested in our societal values since the 1980s The blood-and-guts portrayal perpetrated by the mass media through our televisions newspapers, and magazines glamorizes and creates these false images lusting for drugs, sex, and homicide. This method and/or technique of propagandizing is especially true for blacks in the inner cities, but crosses over to all members of American society,

It is, however, very unfortunate that Afrikan Americans are disproportionately both perpetrators and victims of criminal violence. Afrikan Americans make up over half the country's prison admissions. Nearly one in four Afrikan American men between the ages of twenty and twenty-nine are in prison, on parole, or on probation And homicide is the leading cause of death among Afrikan American youth. Says Marian Wright Edelman, President of the Children's Defense Fund, "We lose more Afrikan American men to guns in our cities in one year than we did during the entire civil war."

As a result of the upsurge in the number of new admissions in the jails and prisons across America, along with the cry for more jails and prisons, minorities constitute a real threat and a liability to the status quo. And their investment in building new prisons and hiring more police to "police" the corrupt police is indeed an example of an inept justice system. All the monies which would ordinarily go into the defense fund have been earmarked for the Justice Department via the courts, police, and prisons. The status quo should be worrying and preparing for the inevitable "Atticas" to erupt across the country in the next three to five years due in part to overcrowding, a dismantling of certain privileges—e.g. weights, televisions, cigarettes—and the cruel and unusual punishment "prisons" such as Pelican Bay in California. A Ninth Circuit judge ruled in favor of inmates who have been subjected to beatings with weapons at Pelican Bay. Guards have been accused of using cruel and unusually excessive means to punish inmates. An unidentified inmate was put in scalding hot water, while also it has been reported that other inmates at Pelican Bay have been killed mysteriously or have committed suicide.

The only good coming out of this "lock the door and throw away the key" mentality is that the inmate earning wage will increase. I foresee small companies who cannot compete with major corporations in the community will contract out with prison industries. The wages for inmates will reach minimum wage by the end of this century. Afrikan American Youths from the ages of fourteen through seventeen who are charged with "certain crimes" will be tried as adults. Some states are sending even younger felons to the adult system at the tender ages of twelve and thirteen. The system labels these children "perpetrators" and "predators" of crime. I conclude they are merely victims of a violent breed of negative images reinforced into their innocent minds (brainwashing) since childhood, having spent the majority of their free time absorbing and falsely personifying these unrealistic characters (e.g. "Beavis and Butthead," "Power Rangers," "King of the Hill," "South Park," "Mantis," gangster rap, "New Jack City," "Scar Face," etc.). In essence, it is a breeding ground of poverty and generations of dysfunctional family systems which account for broken marriages and broken homes, drug users and drug dealers, alcohol use and alcohol abuse, guns and violence, and an especially high incidence of spousal abuse. Ironically, this has brought forth a violent breed of killer-instinct youths who are totally out of control.

There has been a steady increase in juvenile crime in the most serious categories: murder, rape, robbery, and aggravated assault. Homicide arrests of children ages ten through fourteen rose from 194 to 301 between 1988 and 1992. During any one-year period, on a typical day, there are about 100,000 juveniles incarcerated across the country. What do these children have in common with other juveniles across the country? Most of these children have immediate relatives who are or have been incarcerated or who have gone through "the rite of passage." Many of their parents are drug users and/or either present or past criminals. My diagnosis of the "conduct-disordered" juveniles I have interviewed is consistent with an *Apathetic Personality Disorder* children showing signs of an emotionally cold person, devoid of empathy, impulsive, and showing no signs of interests or goal orientation. The prognosis is poor at best. Prognostically, they will land in the penitentiary by the age of sixteen or in the grave by twenty-one. It is an overwhelming relief to know that most of our children do not fall into this forsaken catchment. Therefore, it is imperative to communicate with our children and monitor their activities (with discretion of course) and screen their entertainment devices (TV., movies, music, internet access). This can be done without intruding into their private space. We must become mentors of children as well as parents who only find time to find fault, criticize, and discipline. Get involved with your children's goals, ideals, and dreams.

According to an article written by Gail Russell Chaddock of the Christian Science Monitor, more than 5.6 million Americans are in prison or have served time there, according to a new report by the Justice Department. That's one in thirty-seven adults living in the United States, the highest incarceration level in the world.

If current trends continue, it means that a black male in the United States would have about a one in three chance of going to prison during his lifetime. For a Hispanic male, it's one in six; for a white male, one in seventeen.

These new numbers are shocking enough, but what we don't see are the ripple effects of what they mean: for the generation of black children today, there's almost an inevitable aspect of going to prison. According to the director of the Sentencing Project, a nonprofit advocacy group based in Washington, "We have the wealthiest society in human history, and we maintain the highest level of imprisonment. It's striking what that says about our approach to social problems and inequality."

By the end of year 2001, some 1,319,000 adults were confined in state or federal prisons. An estimated 4,299,000 former prisoners are still alive, the new report concludes. The impact of incarceration does not end with the sentence. Former inmates can be excluded from receiving public assistance, living in public housing, or receiving financial aid for college. Ex-felons are prohibited from voting in many states. And with the increased use of background checks—especially since 9/11—they may be permanently locked out of jobs in many professions, including education, child care, driving a bus, or working in a nursing home.

Enfranchisement for Ex-Felons

More than 4 million prisoners or former prisoners are denied a right to vote; in twelve states, that ban is for life. Some states are already scaling back prohibitions or limits on voting affecting former inmates, including Maryland, Delaware, New Mexico, and Texas. In addition, critics say that efforts to purge voting rolls of former felons could lead to abuse, and effectively disenfranchise many minority voters.

"On the day of the 2000 [presidential] election, there were an estimated 600,000 former felons who had completed their sentence yet because of Florida's restrictive laws, were unable to vote," says Mr. Mauer of the Sentencing Project.

The prison population has quadrupled since 1980. Much of that surge is the result of public policy, such as the war on drugs and mandatory minimum sentencing. Nearly one in four of the inmates in federal and state prisons are there because of drug-related offenses, most of them nonviolent.

Narcotic-Related Arrests

New drug policies have especially affected incarceration rates for women, which have increased at nearly double the rate for men since 1980. Nearly one in three women in prison today are serving sentences for drug-related crimes.

"A lot of people think that the reason crime rates have been dropping over the past several years is, in part, because we're incarcerating the people most likely to commit crimes," says Stephan Thernstrom, a historian at Harvard University.

Others say the drop has more to do with factors such as a generally healthy economy in the 1990s, more opportunity for urban youth, or better community policing. But no one disagrees that prison experience will be a part of the lives of more and more Americans. By 2010, the number of American residents in prison or with prison experience is expected to jump to 7.7 million, or 3.4 percent of all adults, according to the new report.

SOCIOLOGY OF THE FAMILY

The reasons for the increase in violent crimes are multi-faceted, but the starting point is directly related to economics. The rewards for honest work for the less educated have declined and either the jobs are abroad, designated for cheap labor, or pay sub-standard wages. Anyway, the point is, the payoff for crime has risen. Crime does pay in many instances. The explosive drug trade and other illegal pursuits offer jobs, good money, and glamour. According to Richard B. Freeman, an economist at Harvard University, and Harry W. Holzer, an economist at Michigan State University, the wage and employment opportunities have declined dramatically, and opportunities in the criminal sector have grown proportionately.

In addition, the sharp decline of the two-parent family is directly related to the crime problem. Young Afrikan American males resent and harbor negative feelings toward older Afrikan American men mainly because of the lack of direct male bonding or the unavailability or lack of role models to interact with, reflect, or model. Many young Afrikan American criminals are devastating many inner cities and suburban communities, and throwing these people into jail for short periods of time only seems to make matters worse in the long run. Some families are headed by women, and the figure increases significantly in inner-city neighborhoods. A very large part of the decline in marriage rates is traceable to male joblessness and poverty levels. The old, traditional American welfare system encourages female-headed households by providing financial support to unmarried American mothers. American mothers need government-sponsored jobs, not government-sponsored welfare dependence.

Did you know that Afrikan Americans in the United States are the world's only legally created ethnic group? Namely, through the thirteenth, fourteenth, and fifteenth amendments, which can be repealed at any moment by Congress or declared unconstitutional by the Supreme Court. However, with the continuing increase of Afrikan Americans and other minorities entering the political arena and economical elite via the government and privately-owned businesses, we can be assured that this will not occur inasmuch as we need to ensure that our Afrikan American, Caucasian, Hispanic, Native American, Hawaiian, and Asian leaders are aware and active in the daily struggle for humanity against oppression and exploitation.

Our leaders need to ensure that the professionals in whom we place our faith are acting responsibly. For instance, our health professionals are the largest group of "legal" drug pushers. They prescribe unneeded and dangerous drugs along with performing unnecessary operations.

The one constant in this ever-changing world is the ever-present behavior of our leaders in their relationships with minorities. This is a very awkward and very challenging problem, and the inevitable question is, "What should the people do?"

Afrikan Americans and other American minorities must accept the reality that our leaders, democracy, and racial/ethnic oppression are not conflicting ideals. The fact that Afrikan Americans were enslaved for over 350 years by a democratic form of government should be evidence enough. Furthermore, a democratic government possesses an inherent equality of races, therefore it does not provide methods of liberation for those who are not treated equally. However, our Constitution clearly states that "all men should be treated equal."

Therefore, we must move past these self-imposed boundaries and begin to use the resources made available in order to build an everlasting foundation of strong moral and ethical standards for our future generations. The Afrikan American churches, i.e., Afrikan Methodist Episcopal, has stood at least 200 years of trials and tribulations, in addition to outside racist turmoil, because of its strong and secure foundation. Individual members committed to a collective support network have played a great role in protecting the church's continued existence. The churches and temples are an outward expression of our powerful and positive influence on generations of Afrikan Americans. It is by far the largest example of Afrikan American solidarity.

In any attempt to analyze new perspectives for young people in the millennium, it is very important to address the notion of protecting our youth from the many social ills which have literally destroyed the most important universal and moral aspect of our society, the, family. Families have been destroyed by the disparity in the equality of the jobs and education and the disappearance of the monogamous relationship (two parents living in the same household).

Make no inference—I am not putting down or disrespecting single-parent households. To the contrary, most single parents are doing a far better job or at least an equal amount of a superb task of raising a family and serving needs of these families without two-party parents. However, we need fathers who want to be dads, to spend time with their children to guide them and support them with their ideas, goals, and aspirations. We need to rekindle the monogamous relationship. We need to re-:make the extended family. In essence, we need to care for our elderly just *as* we take responsibility for the care of our young children. The disappearance of family values is detrimental for the sustaining of mankind and civilization.

As of today, most of our youth are filled with despair and apathy. We need to stress the importance of good family values. We must encourage our youth to focus on the future. It is theirs to behold.

Suicide is a terrible antidote for addressing our social and personal problems. It directly affects our families and communities in a very negative way. No one wins in a no-win situation (suicide).

Only education and collective awareness will eradicate drug addiction and alcohol abuse. The only safe and sure way to stop the spread of AIDS is to be extra conscious of the ways to contract as well as combat this terribly deadly disease.

We must be about the business of "practicing what we preach" via our schools, churches, and town meetings. Afrikan Americans and other minorities need to stop killing each other. Do you know that the opposite side of the spectrum from homicide is suicide? Suicide only hurts the people who love the victim more than the victim, who didn't love himself.

We need to invest our monies from the temples, churches, and gracious donations into building, maintaining, and managing community centers that are safe and foster family values, and engage in sisterhood and brotherhood ideals that teach uplifting morals. Young people must be able to freely come to a place and interact in a forum in which he or she can express their concerns and issues inasmuch as they may be unable to disclose to their parents, but may find it easier and more acceptable to disclose and express their personal problems with their own peers.

I think it's fair to say that parents should start or continue to organize community watch groups and get involved with their local school P.T.A. (Parent-Teacher Association). As parents who work all day find it difficult to get involved, since it is easier to find excuses to justify their lack of involvement in community affairs. However, P.T.A. meetings could be held on Saturdays. Our solutions to our rationalization of not having time must become proactive in scope and creative in time management. We need to exploit our selfish talents, skills, and abilities amongst ourselves to generate a collective and safe environment where we work, live, and play. Every citizen must be involved and held accountable for the positive growth of our communities.

RACE OR RACISM

Nowadays, anyone can be a racist. Racism has traditionally been tied to the Caucasian race for obvious reasons. But to move forward into the twenty-first century It Is profitable to recognize any person of color may in fact be a racist. A functional definition of racism is: "The oppression and exploitation of people because of their race by another exclusive race." In addition to the latter, there exists an even more subtle form of covert racism. We need to pay very close attention to our leaders. And pay particular attention to the "genocidal" substances and devices absorbing our communities, e.g. population control (abortion and birth control), tobacco, illicit drugs, H.I.V. syndrome, high rates of incarceration, mandatory minimum sentences, and legislative racism (Proposition 187).

It is pathological for Afrikan Americans to keep attempting to use moral suasion on a people, for the most part, who have no morality where race is the variable. Because of their seeming lack of ethical or moral development, there is no conflict between the ruling classes values and racial oppression. The ruling class has historically oppressed, exploited, and killed Afrikan American people and other races of color. A recent article in the *Oakland Tribune,* via the Associated Press, stated "History teaches blacks to mistrust authority." Qubilah Shabazz, the daughter of Malcolm X, was charged with plotting to arrange for the assassination of Louis Farrakhan of the Nation of Islam. However, shocking to the elite establishment perpetrated by the ruling class, the Islam leader defended the accused and castigated the authorities. He asserted that the plot was a government plot to undermine Afrikan American unity. "There is a genuine distrust and it's well earned," said Zakkondo, author of *Conspiracies: Unraveling the Assassination of Malcolm X* and a professor at Bowie State University in Maryland. "They know how the judicial system works. They know what police brutality is, they know what discrimination is.... Other circles can point to concrete examples of government prosecution. They cite documented FBI harassment of Martin Luther King Jr., Malcolm X, and the Black Panthers in the 1960's."

An editorial by Brenda Payton (*Oakland Tribune*) examined the lack of respect accorded to an Afrikan American based only on the color of his skin: "An Afrikan student just recently decided to test it in a modern-day repeat of the 1959 'Black Like Me' experiment. A twenty-one-year-old University of Maryland student started taking Psorlen, a medication that adds melanin and darkens the skin. The student only lasted one week. He stated 'When I changed the color of my skin, I didn't get that respect. Suddenly I had to prove I wasn't a criminal or ignorant or some kind of malcontent. Black people have to constantly prove they are worthy of respect. That's what I couldn't stand.' The student further went on to say the experience was depressing and awful. 'I don't see the willingness of white people to face it. I hate to say it's unconscious because it almost lets us off the hook. But the white superior attitude is so deeply rooted, so ingrained, it's almost invisible.' Conclusively, he states, 'We can't eradicate racism. But at least if we come to terms with it, we can check it.'"

In yet another editorial by Brenda Payton, she addressed instances of obvious institutional racism: "Wealthy Afrikan Americans are turned down for home loans at a higher rate than low-to-medium income whites. In several studies, Afrikan American job applicants matched perfectly with white applicants."

We've made progress in thirty years, but racial prejudice is still very much with us, especially in the hands of politicians and judges. The income gaps between Afrikan Americans and whites reflect its endurance—Afrikan American college graduates still make less than whites who only completed high school." We still must redress continued racial discrimination. Otherwise we'll lose ground that we've gained in our progress toward racial equality.

THEORY OR LIBERATION

We the people, as Afrikan Americans and other minorities, must be about the sincere business of liberating the minds of our children, but first we must accept the responsibility of disengaging ourselves from the shackles of our own individual mental oppression. One cannot expect to teach higher learning if one denies herself or himself the opportunity to learn higher education and uphold moral values.

I propose the starting point for developing a multi-cultural social theory begins in the home. It is the parents' obligation to teach these concepts just as it is important to teach morals, manners, and social skills to our children. The remaining balance of these proposed social theory concepts should be reinforced in our schools, e.g. prayer or three to five minutes of silent inner reflection. The churches or temples have the responsibility of teaching appropriate virtues: moral excellence and righteousness.

A social theory determines the destiny of a people, establishing objectives and guidelines for their existence. It also defines values and rituals, methods of child-rearing, education, etc.

By putting this theory into action, the best safeguard is using the pulpit as the vehicle of operation. The churches and the temples are the most powerful functioning network to put this multi-cultural theory into real practice. The churches and temples should never be held in a vacuum. The congregation needs to be taught not about the religion of Jesus, but the religion (way of life) that Jesus taught to his apostles and disciples. The Muslims do not need to be taught about the religion of Mohammed but they need to be taught how to live righteously like Mohammed, the prophet of Islam. The ultimate components of achieving a multi-cultural theory would be the existence of a morally conscious lifestyle, freedom to choose, self-determination, and dignity of the recognition and reintegration of a nation-wide multi-culturally society accepted by all its citizens.

South Africa, its newly established democracy, should take the lead role in implementing and developing an international integrative, multicultural society if they intend to save face with the modern world. This coalition of newly elected officials in the new government of South Afrika should preserve the ideal of a free world. South Africa's example could be a model for all other nations to follow to preserve the human race. The human race, all of God's children, are created equal regardless of those individual handicaps that separate us from being the same. We are still created by one outstanding creator (God).

It is disturbing and unbelievable that Afrikan Americans and other American minorities continue to ignore an irrefutable truth, namely, that in a racist social system, all institutions will reflect, project, perpetuate, and sustain values that are consistent with institutional racism, e.g., judiciary, legislative, higher education, and the most powerful, the media (newspapers, TV. news, and radio). This should not be surprising or profound, since all institutions serve to perpetuate the social theory of the group which created them. Therefore, in order to liberate the minds of American minorities men, women, and children, a multi-cultural theory must be realized not only as an ideal dream but a reality.

Dr. Cheika Anta Diop, an Afrikan American scientist, succinctly placed culture in its proper perspective by stating the following: "I consider culture as rampart which protects a people, a collectivity. Culture must, above all, play a protective role. It must ensure the cohesion of the group. Following this line of thinking, the vital functions of a body of Afrikan human sciences is to develop this sense of collective belonging through a reinforcement of culture. This can be done by developing the linguistic factors, by reestablishing the historical consciousness of Afrikan people so as to arrive at a common feeling of belonging to the same cultural and historic past."

Once this is attained, it will be difficult to divide and rule and to set Afrikan American communities against each other. We need to practice the "share" concept and to love thy neighbor as one loves thyself. More specifically, the haves vs. the have-nots and the Christians vs. the Muslims. This negative depreciation must end now.

We as a united front of multi-cultural people must be about the serious business of examining our struggle as collective. Although we may have separate racist issues to tackle we still have one common agenda— free speech and free enterprise. Our goal is to be free of exploitation and oppression by an elite "corporate" ruling class.

There is no other resolution for liberation.

True, Afrikan American ancestors were stolen from Afrika and sold, but to keep one's mind in bondage after so many years of quasi-freedom in America is counter-productive thinking. This kind of mentality is in the root of slavery. It is guided by a false sense of spirituality—we need to reject this "blame the victim" syndrome and move forward with a liberated mind-set (no excuses).

In the '50s, '60s, and '70s Afrikan Americans fought the adversaries of discrimination. These were the periods of the late great Civil Rights Movements Malcolm X to Dr. Martin Luther King, not to mention Sir John Brown, Ms. Sojouner Truth, Mr. Fredrick Douglass Mr. W.E.B. Dubosis, Mr. Marcus Garvey, the "Black" Muslims and the former Black Panther Party. It is a pity the late Huey P. Newton was not able to transcend his dream beyond the scope of the "inner city blues."

The Honorable Elijah Mohammed and his successor, one of the greatest twentieth century orators, the Honorable Louis Farrakhan, never receive worldwide acceptance, despite the fact they both offered the most powerful economic base and self-help program to date for Afrikan men, women, and children.

Albeit, the future will offer an extremely serious challenge to all American minorities and particularly Afrikan Americans since they hold a considerable stock in American investments, having access to incredible capital because of their individual superstardom, e.g. Oprah Winfrey, Michael Jackson, Michael Jordan, Eddie Murphy, Whitney Houston, Johnson Publishing Company, Bill Cosby, Deon Sanders, Diana Ross, Brian Gumble, etc. The list is endless. However, it is quite unfortunate that this group can't rebuild our communities and tear down the ghettos and create jobs with all their capital. These people's net worth together could rid us of 90 percent of the problems associated with poverty. It is better to give than to receive. These people need to not be so selfish and invest in our youth's future. **The only person that I know who has invested in the youth is Oprah Winfrey. She has the insight into our youths' futures and also in our future political direction by supporting Barack Obama.**

As American minorities, we must command the attention of this drug-invested perversion of America and take back the streets of this modern-day Babylon with our own voice and with our fire power. I need not waste your time and mine on elaborating on the definition of "fire power."

As Malcolm once said, "By any means necessary." We must take the time (time out) and instill in the minds of our youth the great morals and values that sit in final judgment of our Father. To want less is to accept these evils of temptation and manifestations of racism that have continued and will continue to shackle our minds and our agenda. The Reverend Jesse Jackson puts it in another way: "Anyone who can define you can also confine you."

EDUCATION: PRIVATE OR PUBLIC

P arents need to take over the school system from state government. No one needs to remain in denial. Caucasians, Afrikan Americans, minorities, we all must come together for the good of all mankind, to take action and liberate our children from the shackles of the public school system. Today's classrooms all seem to resemble a horror show in some respect. The public school system has failed its students. This crisis is just another inherent failure of our racist society. The teachers do not have the time nor the resources to give each student individual attention, therefore the children are not given special instruction nor being taught independently of their own worth. Probably before year's end most teachers are burnt out not for teaching purposes but for lack of educational resources and safe environments. The wear and tear of teaching in some heavy-duty war zones (bad neighborhoods) takes a pounding on a good, dedicated teacher. But because of low salary gaps and the lack of protection and inept school boards, the problems still persist. Sooner or later, albeit sooner, most teachers will give up the "blackboard jungle" in hopes and search of some new locations.

Some of the schools that I have visited in the last couple of years are so physically degraded, one might think he has driven up to a penitentiary or a reform school. Graffiti is everywhere, children are hanging out smoking cigarettes and Pakololo (marijuana), kicking it with gangster rap.

Some of the children I have interviewed express fear and apprehension about going to school, fear of being assaulted, molested, and extorted by their peers and/or adversaries. Most schools today have an abundance of security precautions, e.g. metal detectors, cameras, security personnel, and dogs. Some schools entertain undercover vice. But even in the light of these high-tech security devices there is still too much incidence of violence perpetuated day in and day out in our public school system. At present, our school systems, via the traditional teaching principles are a failure. There is solid proof that these ancient modes of teaching are depressing and yoking.

Our children are systematically being engaged in a redundant and inferior mode of teaching, reading, writing, arithmetic, English, and social studies. Exposing these public school children to fairy tales—Columbus discovered America, Afrikan Americans have no valuable history and contributions to the American agenda, and the Indians started or created all the wars against the cavalry and the white man—are a distortion and blatant lie.

In addition to the lies and distortions of American history, our children are exposed to an inferior academic curriculum. When comparing our children with other world children and giving them standardized tests with the same amount of time allotted to finish these tests, students from Canada, Europe, and Asia outsmarted our children in all areas. Our children are becoming extremely bored at school by no later than the fourth and fifth grades. These promising children are stifled by the inferior and redundant methods of teaching. They become distracted, disinterested, aggressive, and frustrated with school. At best our classrooms become day care centers while the teachers become the child care providers, babysitting our children while the parents go to work. Very little is being taught and hardly anything is being absorbed. No wonder kids are bringing guns to school for show and tell.

What is happening at some schools in some neighborhoods is an outright destruction aimed at our children's minds. (Shame on us.) Our academic standards are weak at the public school level and there is hardly any enthusiastic progression toward competitive and challenging educational goals in most of our school districts.

In order to liberate scores of undernourished children from the slavery of public education and a systematic racist curriculum, we must create and develop our own privatized schools. Home schooling along with self-taught principles sounds like the safe bet. However, it is extremely important not just to bail out of a degrading school system but to hold county and city government accountable for this embarrassment and failure.

As members of our churches and temples, we readily have access to our own capital. We can use our building funds and generous offerings from our constituents in our churches, parishes, temples, and fraternities. We must elect and hire our teachers from within our community organizations to oversee and implement our school community-based management schools. Students will be taught about the immorality of drug use and drug abuse, sex abstinence and sex education—e.g. safe sex, contraceptives, planned parenthood, individual and group counseling, AIDS education—violence awareness and gang prevention, social skills (ethics), and etiquette. Television should be controlled by responsible parenting. We should readily take on and extract from the private school concept of dress—shirt, tie, and dress slacks for boys and appropriate uniform dress for girls. Our educators should teach about the different religions of the world. A moral and ethical education must be taught. We certainly need to go back to the business of prayer in school or at least a moment of silence for self-reflection. Education opens the door for truth-seeking students who should know God, and worship God, not materialism. Racist capitalism and the American dollar are the root of all evil. All those things will come to pass. However, faith seekers will find eternal life, peace, and contentment.

My brothers, my sisters, do not be overwhelmed by these nontraditional concepts. The present education system is not working out to our benefit. Remember, we already have great colleges and universities in existence which are owned and operated by Afrikan Americans and other minorities.

And out of these universities we already produce some of the most articulate and talented students in the world. I sincerely believe we should act at once; we need to set up privately owned day care, pre school care, grammar schools, and high school programs in each of our separate communities.

We need to take back the schools from the state, if we expect our children to learn how to be responsible adults. These concepts are not impossible. To continue down the same path is a nightmare...and means eventual destruction of moral and social values.

ECONOMICS: INVESTING IN OUR FUTURE

Afrikan Americans and other minorities in the United States must invest their monies in overseeing of the major share of the mass media, e.g. radio, television, and newspapers, but excluding the entertainment field. We need to concentrate on education and business ventures. Afrikan Americans and other American minorities have to continue to gather, disseminate, and report by minority-owned media enterprises.

This will enable us to control the ramifications of freedom of speech. To allow your present ruling class adversaries to exclusively dominate the media guarantees that you will lose the effectiveness in reaching out and communicating news.

The "movement" is alive and fortified but we still need to recruit (solid) disciples who can represent the issues and concerns of the masses. Our people of color are of diversified cultures meaning we accept and acknowledge all third-world people, Afrikans, Hispanics, Native Americans, Eskimos, Samoans, Hawaiians, Filipinos, West Indians, South Americans, Muslims, and other revolutionaries. We all have the same common goal in the long haul, and that is to save our children from self-destruction.

Many very competent minorities who are naive about their own historical contributions to society have more often than not, flunked out of schools because of the independent insistence of studying the etiology of their ethnicity. Minority students must be taught and realize that the "ruling class" ownership (board of regents) and their governorship of these Ivy league educational institutions are the oppressors' turf that protects them from relating to or understanding the minorities life-long contributions as well as the historic input to the growth and expansionism of modernization. To deny this exposes an unthinkable depth of psychology and sociology.

Randall Robinson expounded in an article in *Ebony* magazine that, "Things don't happen because they are right. Things happen because tenacious people keep their promises, and if they do not, are prepared, ready and able, and committed to exacting a political cost."

Precisely. What I hear Robinson saying is for the ruling class to change their opinion toward Afrikan Americans and other American minorities is to affect their fortunes—pocketbook fortunes.

We the people, as American minorities, need to invest in American interests that are best served by the general population, but we also need to invest in cross-cultural ventures in the Caribbean and South Africa. Today, with Apartheid dead and gone, the new democracy of South Africa becomes a "prime" investment for Afrikan Americans in all areas relating to academics, education, economics, and society.

South Africa is extremely rich in minerals and resources. Afrikan Americans should be readily assessable and venture over to Africa and join in the struggle and become the backbone of helping to socially restructure and rebuild an integrationist South Africa.

I am confident that the majority of South Afrikans will welcome our input with open arms if we leave our selfish, capitalistic, distorted indoctrinations back in America. Our past experiences with the Civil Rights Movement and redevelopment period of reconstruction of the '70s and '80s will allow us to share our vast skills and abilities to this relatively new form of democracy with equal jobs, equal pay, equal free speech, and equal liberties. As disciples of the late Civil Rights Movement, we can take great pride in our role in the liberation of South Africa. Long live Mandela, a warrior who was destined to be chief.

As Richard Hatcher stated in an article in *Ebony*, "It is not simply to be politically equal, but it is imperative that we become economically equal as well." The general population must begin to operate and own America's economy and businesses so that we can avoid the pitfalls of the ruling class racist exploitations. As of today, it can be said, "We are living in a capitalistic country, but we have very little capital."

Apathy or Strategy

Afrikan Americans and other American minorities must always remember and never forget their early exclusion and disenfranchisement from the elite-class politics and economic investments.

The principle challenge for all minorities regardless of economic status is to boycott and denounce institutional racism and mass-media control by a select group of elite conglomerates.

As concerned citizens we should organize community watch groups and run the drug dealers out of town by any means necessary. We must seize the opportunity and reclaim our communities and rebuild them with love and neighborly concerns for sisterhood and brotherhood. We need to cast out the demons of gang mentality in our children and instill religious morals and values that are the same in the long haul. Secondly, having accomplished this goal, we should exercise our right in establishing a powerful networking scheme that will involve the churches, temples, and prisons. We will call this scheme the "Revolutionary Triangle," bible study being one of the vehicles to address our concerns of the poor, oppressed, and non-believers.

In addition to proactive Bible studies, we should elicit the best advertisers, best educated, and best money managers to reinvest in our home communities. By gaining interests and capital from our individual property holdings we can tear down dilapidated housing projects, which the elite refer to as "ghettos," a ghetto being defined as a section of a city to which an ethnic or economically depressed minority group is *restricted,* as by poverty or social pressure racism. "Restricted" in the sense of not attaining college or financial support; hence leaving generations of welfare, drug abuse, and drug-dealing infested environments to infest and perpetuate into the twenty-first century.

Believe it or not, we do not need the Affirmative Action Program as it presently exists. We do, however, need an agency to keep a watch dog on company hiring practices. If found in violation of practicing unfair and racist employment practices, we should fine them and court order these companies or agencies to fix the deficiencies immediately or face jail time.

We as minorities want Pell grants reinstated in the penitentiaries. Prisoners need to have access to higher learning. To be undereducated is to be ignorant of your environment. Make no mistake, to cage someone and not to feed him the language then release him from bondage is in itself capital punishment!

Our dilapidated neighborhoods need housing and subsidized grants to relocate families while ghettos are being torn down and replaced with parks and community action centers. The land within the city limits should be contracted out through bidding and appropriate single dwelling homes should be erected on one-quarter acreage tracts. This will alleviate the concrete jungles!"

If the leaders of our country were to become more accountable to their constituents and oversee how this money is being spent to improve the communities and the families who live there, I am confident we can break the dead-end cycle of poverty and despair. We as disciples of our communities have to have more input and say on how to utilize these grants. The state and federal H.U.D. must be held accountable for these restricted war zones, e.g. ghettos, barrios, and Section 8 public housing that have become destructive, drug-infested, rat-infested eyesores that have deteriorated over the years.

As community activists we need to be aware of the hidden agenda by the elite to restrict our movement in the mainstream. Therefore, it is essential and imperative to educate our youth about the man with the plan, the plan being to keep minorities in *check* with welfare and the generational cycle of poverty and despair.

Our youth is our ticket out of the concrete jungle. We need to rid ourselves of this evil diagnosis of "Apathetic Personality Disorder" and fight back to gain the dignity lost to poverty, drugs, and alcohol.

In the final analysis, there must be a major role played by the international Afrikan American community and worldwide religious affiliations that must be committed to democracy in America and elsewhere. Democracy does not only mean access to the electoral process it means ensuring, through shared values and morals, the cultivation of hope and economic prosperity—jobs, not drugs. The Afrikan American, the Hispanic American, the Chinese American,, the Native American—and the list goes on—must make it a number one priority to get rid of the drugs, drug dealers, and youth gang mentality. We must be dead serious about implementing God-fearing morals and values in our children. We must persevere and remain firm, fair, and consistent in our holy determination, and we will prevail. Don't just be a victim in the war against crime and the oppression of our youth.

Government will persist only by artificial famine and insemination of deadly viruses into the mainstream population. Mass imprisonment and mass deportation will be the rule of the world. A really efficient tyranny of government would be one in which the political bosses and the "select" elite will control the masses and the population, who will not have to be whipped or coerced into submission but who will lovingly accept their servitude. To make them love it will be the tasks of the "Newties" and the New World Order and their ministers of propaganda. The greatest achievement will be substituting minds with television, turning individuals into twenty-four-hour couch potatoes armed with remote control. We must reject this servitude and ignite the revolution and overcome them which is of this world.

SAVING OUR YOUTH

A Twelve-Step Plan for the Future

1. Establish a system of social organization. Develop a Neighborhood Watch Group.

2. Join the FAMM Foundation, Families Against Mandatory Minimums (see endnote for address).

3. Establish or join a geographical network that is located in your area and set up a nationwide coalition that addresses the needs of minorities, e.g. political, social, economic, and religious (Million Man March held in October of 1995, Washington, D.C.).

4. Go into the jails, prisons, and detention centers and teach the "Good News Gospel." Adopt an inmate.

5. Join your community church or temple. Give testimony and teach Bible study.

6. Design and distribute a newsletter focusing on the needs of your local community.

7. Establish an endorsement for loans, bail monies, and appropriate investments. Have fundraisers to bring in new recruits, set up town meetings that fit the time schedule for most members in your watch group.

8. Develop and manage a shelter for abused children and a separate one for victims of spousal abuse. Develop and manage a halfway house for men and women getting out of prison, or set up community Big Brother and Big Sister houses that will help phase and reintegrate persons back to civilian life.

9. Develop and oversee an after-school program for pre-teens with an emphasis on sex education, crime prevention, and drug and alcohol awareness.

10. Establish a court referral service to catch potential offenders in detention centers in your community. This referral network can divert clients to halfway houses, shelters, or foster care. All three of these alternatives are better than jail.

11. Establish a twenty-four-hour, seven-day-a-week hotline to assist children in your community who are in crisis because of suicidal identification, sexual abuse, harassment, battered baby syndrome, mental health, drug and alcohol, H.I.V. information, and issues related to teenage pregnancy.

12. Register to vote (participate fully in the local and national election process).

JESUS CHRIST AND THE POOR

The Bible, the Poor, and the Black Church

It is commonplace to hear churchgoers and non-:churchgoers alike repeat the old refrain, "Who is the worst enemy of the poor other than the poor themselves." Whether this statement serves as a rationale or a compensatory resolve as to why the poor should be deserted does little to relieve the Church's responsibility of addressing the needs of the less fortunate. Notwithstanding, as a whole, the non-biblically and theologically trained persons today generally have the insight and understanding that the ministry and teachings of Jesus were primarily devoted to those whose material needs were not sufficient to promote daily comfort and support human survival. One of the quotations of Jesus that stands out the most in reference to the treatment of the poor is, "When I was hungry (beggar) you gave me meat" (Matt. 25:35). This serves as a catalyst to the concept of Christianity, whose principle foundation teaches "brotherly love" or "love thy neighbor as thyself." There are other salient examples, such as the widow's mite and the Beatitudes from the Sermon on the Mount, which authenticates the complete ministry of Jesus as a love-centered religion. During the time of Christ, and even to this day, the poor and misfortunate, widows, the handicapped, the ill, and the destitute were the most oppressed, discriminated, forgotten, and socially downtrodden.

Though the teachings of Christianity and the complete Bible make several references to the slothful, lazy, and carefree persons as examples of self-inflicted poverty, these were not the persons that He often made references to when speaking about the poor. Jesus' heart was directed toward the people whose fate in life gave them no other recourse than to accept a lowly and meaningless way of living. These were the people who had to succumb to those unavoidable circumstances that prevailed over their personal lives. Throughout his brief ministry, Christ left no doubt as to how he stood with the poor: "The least you do unto these my brethren, you do also unto me" (Matt. 25:40).

What is the most dominant biblical understanding of the poor? The Hebrew terms for poor can stand for the materially needy, the socially oppressed, or the spiritually lowly. These primary Hebrew terms are the most significant, because they express most completely the varied characters of the biblical understanding of the poor.

What is astonishing today about the Old Testament position on the poor is that God is consistently depicted as being on their side. Indeed, to help the poor is to help God, and to oppress the poor is to bring about God's condemnation. "He who oppresses the poor shows contempt for his Maker, but whoever is kind to the needy honors God," and "He that hath pity upon the poor lendeth unto the Lord; and that which he hath given will he pay him again" (Prov. 19:17). The Psalmist sums it up when he says "[God] upholds the cause of the oppressed" (Psalm 146:7).

In addition, the Old Testament condemns people for acts of omission against the poor as well as acts of commission. The prophet Amos records God's condemnation of Israel for acts of commission when he says, "They sell the needy for a pair of sandals…. They trample on the heads of the poor as upon the dust of the ground, and deny justice to the oppressed" (Amos 2:6-7a, 5:21-24, 8:1-10). God's condemnation of Israel recorded by Isaiah (similarly Jeremiah) offers us another insight when he says, "It is you who have ruined my vineyard; the plunder from the poor is in your houses. What do you mean by crushing my people and grinding the faces of the poor?" (Is. 3:14-15, Jer.:5:26-29). Old Testament passages like these make it clear that God does not cast down the rich simply because they are rich, but because of the manner in which many of them got their riches (oppression of the poor and at the expense of the poor), and how they use their riches (to maintain their privileged position over the poor).

The latter point highlights the condemnation of omission in helping the poor. One of the most overlooked points in the story of Sodom and Gomorrah is that the people were condemned and destroyed as much for their lack of concern for the poor as for their sexual misconduct. Ezekiel records the words of God on this matter: "Now this was the sin of your sister Sodom: She and her daughters were arrogant, overfed, and unconcerned; they did not help the poor and needy. They were haughty and did detestable things before me. Therefore I did away with them as you have seen" (Ee. 16:49-50, Isa. 1:10-17).

The New Testament is just as consistent as the Old Testament about its understanding of the poor. In fact, it describes the poor in a more restricted, literal way. The key Greek term means the economically poor; those who lack the necessities of life and must beg to get help. Twenty-two out of the twenty-eight times that this term is used in the New Testament it means those economically poor (Mark 10:21, 12:42; Luke 14:5, 16:20, 22; James 2:2-6; John 13:29; Rom. 15:26; 2 Cor. 6:10; Gal. 2:10). Only three times is the term used to mean "spiritually" poor (Matt. 5:3; Gal. 4:9; Rev. 3:17) and these are not relevant to the discussion of what it means to be poor in the New Testament.

There are three other instances that are disputed as to whether they mean spiritually poor or sociologically poor (Luke 4:18, 6:20, 7:22; Matt. 11:5). Major Eurocentric scholars have made every attempt to interpret these three passages to mean spiritually poor in order to take the radicality out of Jesus' statements that announce the good news of the kingdom as a special privilege of the poor.

This is not the context for engaging in that debate. Let a few words suffice. Since all three of these passages appear in Luke's Gospel and it is undeniable that throughout Luke's Gospel, like none of the other Gospels, he has a special interest in the economically poor and all of the other instances in his Gospel are clearly referring to the economically poor it is astounding that these passages should be taken in any other way. Only the affluence of the West and their attempt to justify their sinful ways by reducing the bite of Jesus' statement can explain why many Eurocentric scholars have made every attempt to deny this reality. However, the larger scholarly world is slowly acknowledging that these three New Testament passages, like all the others, refer to the economically poor.

As with the Old Testament, the New Testament makes it clear that God is on the side of the poor and oppressed. Jesus' well-known first sermon, that he came to preach good news to the poor and to release the oppressed and set the captives free, makes this clear (Luke 4:18-19). It is very often that the plight of the poor is due to the greed of the rich. What a radical thought: The poor are singled out as a special group to be recipients of Jesus' gospel in this sermon, preached by the one who came to save the world. Try as much as you will to reduce the force of that special privilege the fact of the matter is that it makes clear that the poor are especially dear to God. Attempts at spiritualizing this text won't work for two reasons: Jesus is quoting Isa. 61:1, which undeniably refers to the material and physical state of the people.

Besides, what Luke writes later (7:18-23) makes it absolutely clear. A little known fact is how the identity of the poor is used in the New Testament to make clear that Jesus is the Messiah. When John the Baptist was in jail, he sent his disciples to ask Jesus if he was really the Messiah; one of the ways that Jesus responded to ensure John that he was the Messiah is when he said, "Tell him that I preach the good news to the poor." Those who were materially in want, as well as those whose spiritual impoverishment, needed assessment (Luke 7:18-23; Matt. 11:1-5). This type of connection is further emphasized by Paul when he said to the Corinthians, "For you know the grace of our Lord Jesus Christ, that though he was rich, yet for your sakes he became poor, so that you through his poverty might become rich" (2 Cor. 8:9). What benefit could this be for the Corinthians unless there was some special privilege perceived to be accorded the poor? Who can deny that Jesus' entire ministry reflects this type of favor toward the poor and oppressed?

The New Testament is just as consistent as the Old in condemning acts of commission and omission of the poor. As with the Old Testament, the New Testament makes it clear also that how one obtains riches and how one uses riches, as opposed to merely having riches, are the basis of condemnation. James is very direct about this matter. "Now listen, you rich people, weep and wail because of the misery that is coming upon you.... You have heaped treasures in the last days.... You have lived on earth in luxury and self-indulgence" 5:1-6; Mark 12:40).

Who can ever forget that graphic portrayal in the parable of the rich man who filled his barns to the top, while showing unconcern for the needs of the poor, and God said to him, "You fool! This very night your life will be demanded from you. Then who will get what you have prepared for yourself? This is how it will be with anyone who stores up things for himself but is not rich toward God" (Luke 12:13-21).

The implication has already been addressed that when you are rich toward the poor, you are rich toward God; thus the reader cannot help but get the force of the message in the parable. Even more pointed, however, is the parable of the rich man and Lazarus (Luke 16). This parable points out that one's treatment of the poor has something to *do* with heaven and hell. It also supports the fact that it is not riches per se, but the callous unconcern for the poor by those who have riches that is at issue in the parable.

All through the Bible then, the poor are taken to be an oppressed group of the economically and the socially deprived, who because they are the victims of oppression will be the beneficiaries of salvation and will mediate this salvation to others.

In light of the biblical understanding of the poor, what does this mean for Christians and the Church? What are their respective responsibilities? It can be said in two words: imitate God. When God's people care for the poor, they imitate God and those who neglect the poor and oppressed are really not God's people at all, no matter how frequent their religious ritual or how orthodox their creeds and confessions.

Although Christians have no individual responsibility to do this, God also calls the corporate community to this task, because they can do more as a group than one person. Notice how Jesus admonished us that when we have a dinner or banquet to invite the poor, and you will be blessed because they cannot repay you. You will be repaid at the resurrection of the just (Luke 14:12-14).

When Israel failed to carry out God's mandates, God not only condemned individuals, God condemned the entire community. Therefore, any church that does not take the poor as a first priority in its mission does not imitate God. Any church that does not prophesy against its own people, as well as all others on this matter, does not imitate God.

One of the most unfortunate things that has happened to the Christian church: in the West is its overemphasis of orthodoxy (doctrine) while de-emphasizing orthopraxy (action). The fact of the matter is that the Bible says just as much about the treatment of the poor as the true measure of Christianity as it does about the belief in the Resurrection. Because so many today have sold themselves to the God of materialism in the West, it has become necessary to perform a kind of theological gymnastics that would allow one to insulate oneself from this biting indictment.

The church is supposed to be the repository of God's word, the model of God's plan of reconciliation for a broken world, and the incarnational extension of Jesus Christ in the world. Jesus said that because he goes to his Father, we would do even greater works than he did (John 14:12). We should take note of an interesting set of circumstances in the early church; as a result of their imitating Jesus, the record in Acts says that, "There was not a needy person among them" (Acts 4:34).

Proper understanding of economic justice, treatment of the poor, and the kingdom of God cannot be taught anywhere other than the Church, because it is the Bible that presents God's position on the matter, and it is the Church that God has charged with the responsibility of interpreting, preaching, and teaching this Word. It is on the basis of the Word that the Church can invoke the words of I John to prove that treatment of the poor is a key measure of true Christianity when it says, "If anyone has the world's good and sees his brother in need, yet closes his heart against him, how does God's love abide in him? Little children, let us not love word or speech but in deed and in truth" (I John 3:17-18). Note again the emphasis in this passage: The condemnation is not due to something that was done, but something that wasn't done—a sin of omission.

Apart from the prophetic witness and the call to repentance by the Church, it is not possible to persuade people to change because human nature as it is seeks to do its will, not God's will. Only the Church can stand in the gap between self-centeredness and other-centeredness and recite the words of Luke with power: **"Woe to you that are rich; woe to you that are full now; woe to you that laugh now; and blessed are you that hunger now; blessed are you that weep now; blessed are you poor, for yours is the kingdom of God" (Luke 6:20-26). No one, absolutely no one, can level that prophecy but the Church.**

Now then, what does this have to do with economic development in the Black Church? One does not have to be a genius to figure out that few individual blacks in this country, whether Christian or non-Christian, are in a position to make major economic differences in the plight of the masses of black people. It is also self-evident that white people in this country, Christian and non-Christian, are demanding that less and less of their tax dollars be given to blacks.

We must never forget that God has been concerned with the plight of black folks throughout history in a way that makes them uniquely capable

of addressing the problem of the poor. First, when God selected what is referred to as his "chosen people," they were a band of poor slaves residing on the continent of Africa. Second, when God decided to take on flesh and model what it meant to care for the poor, He took on Afro-Asiatic body. Third, when God decided to move the gospel into the Gentile world, he *did* so first through a black Ethiopian who was himself rich, but was transformed into one who cared enough about the masses of black people that he spread the good news to the masses that had to include the poor. Henceforth, when God decided to bring America face-to-face with her worst sin, the enslavement of God's people, the black Church was chosen to provide many leaders.

Furthermore, when God made it possible for Afrikan Americans to gain their freedom in America and remain free, he gave them the black Church. It has been the only institution that was totally black controlled and used as a sanctuary of freedom. Throughout the history of this country the black Church and black religious leaders have been the primary vanguards for Afrikan Americans in the struggle for freedom and justice. The black Church has been that impregnable fortress, that inviolable sanctuary where the afflicted masses found solace and sanity, in the midst of insanity; a place where those whose identity, has been violated could have their identity reaffirmed, a tabernacle of God where continuity could be maintained in the midst of radical discontinuity.

Then, if economic development is to begin en masse, what better place than the black Church? Though the average person in the black Church may not be rich and may not have much, no other black corporate body in America can match what is taken in collectively, Sunday after Sunday in black churches. If it can be understood that condemnation falls upon God's church that does not treat the poor properly, and that lack of action on behalf of the poor falls into that category; perhaps the Church will also understand that economic development is a necessity.

Likewise, in light of God's rejection of the worship of his people who were not actively trying to do something about the plight of the poor and oppressed, the black Church must also learn that God feels the same way about it. When will the budgets, the ministries, indeed, the very fabric and structure of the church, reflect the same sense of concern for the poor that God requires throughout the whole scripture and salvation-history? We are to be actively seeking every way possible to snatch the poor out of the jaws of poverty, to break their yoke of oppression, and lift them to the heights of dignity. How can we do that if we are not actively involved in economic ministries that help them to become independent and interdependent? Are we not involved in helping to perpetuate another form of slavery, the slavery of religiosity?

"Hear, O black Church, why God" condemns the worship of Israel, his people: "Why have we fasted, they say, and [God] has not seen it? Why have we humbled ourselves, and you have not noticed—Is this what you call a fast, a day acceptable to the Lord? Is not this the kind of fasting I have chosen to loose the chains of injustice and untie the cords of the yoke, to set the oppressed free and break every yoke? Is it not to share your food with the hungry and to provide the poor wanderer with shelter, when you see the naked, to clothe him, and not to turn away from your own flesh and blood?... And if you spend yourselves in behalf of the hungry and satisfy the needs of the oppressed, then your light will rise in the darkness, and your night will become like the noonday" (Isa. 58:3-10).

These are the words of Isaiah that bring us to our final question. What does this have to do with the kingdom of God? It is noteworthy that Jesus picks up this very thought as he tells his disciples a parable which explains the ultimate judgment: "When the Son of Man comes in his glory, and all the angels with him, he will sit on his throne in heavenly glory. All the nations will be gathered before him, and he will separate the people one from another as a shepherd separates the sheep from the goats. He will put the sheep on his right and the goats on his left."

"Then the King will say to those on his right, Come, you who are blessed by my Father; take your inheritance, the kingdom prepared for you since the creation of the world. For I was hungry and you gave me something to eat, I was thirsty and you gave me something to drink, I was a stranger and you invited me in, I needed clothes and you clothed me, I was sick and you looked after me, I was in prison and you came to visit me."

"Then the righteous will answer him, Lord, when did we see you hungry and feed you, or thirsty and give you something to drink? When did we see you a stranger and invite you in, or needing clothes and clothe you? When did we see you sick or in prison and go to visit you?"

"The King will reply, I tell you the truth, whatever you did for one of the least of these brothers of mine, you did for me."

"Then he will say to those on his left, Depart from me, you who are cursed, into the eternal fire prepared for the devil and his angels. For I was hungry and you gave me nothing to eat, I was thirsty and you gave me nothing to drink, I was a stranger and you did not invite me in, I needed clothes and you did not clothe me, I was sick and in prison and you did not look after me."

"They will answer, Lord, when did we see you hungry and thirsty or a stranger or needing clothes or sick or in prison, and did not help you?"

"He will reply, I tell you the truth, whatever you did not do for one of the least of these, you did not do for me."

"Then they will go away to eternal punishment, but the righteous to eternal life" (Matt. 25:31-46).

There have been many sermons, articles, and books on what determines whether or not one is truly Christian and what will be the basis of the final judgment. Is it possible that the treatment of the poor is the ultimate test of true Christianity? This is a timeless question that each generation must wrestle with afresh.

The Truth about Religion

Jesus did not incarnate in the likeness of mortal flesh and bestow himself upon the humanity of Earth to reconcile an angry God, but rather to win all mankind to the recognition of the Father's love and to the reality that Jesus is in fact the Son of God.

In order for society to flourish and persist, religion must become a forceful influence for moral stability and spiritual progression functioning internationally in the midst of these ever-changing disturbing conditions and never-ending economic fluctuations.

Religion is born out of the sincere desire to love God and to love every man, woman, and child as his brother. Religion thus becomes the highest social order of mankind, that in which man loves his neighbor as he loves himself. Thus the only appropriate attitude for mankind is the teaching of non-violence, the doctrine of peaceful evolution in the place of violent revolution.

If you can comprehend true religion, you can understand the concept of "Heaven." The Kingdom of Heaven is neither a social nor economic order. Truthfully speaking, it is an exclusively spiritual brotherhood of God-knowing individuals.

Religion becomes genuine and worthwhile if it fosters in the individual an experience in which the sovereignty of truth, beauty, and goodness prevails, for such is the true spiritual concept of supreme reality. Through love and worship, this becomes meaningful as fellowship with man and sonship with God.

The truth about religion is to know God as your Father and man as your brother. Religion is effective in spiritualizing the believer and will have powerful consequences in the social order of the day. The religion that transformed out of Jesus' teachings is the most dynamic influence ever to activate the human race. Even Louis Farrakhan acknowledges this truth when teaching the masses.

The purpose of religion is to magnify the universal truths of beauty, goodness and brotherhood, to foster the attractions of supreme values, to enhance the service of fellowship, to strengthen family life, to promote religious education, to provide wise counsel and spiritual guidance. Finally, the purpose of religion is to encourage group worship, human friendship, conserve morality, promote neighborhood welfare, and facilitate the spread of the "Good News."

Mankind will never wisely decide temporal issues or transcend the selfishness of personal interests unless he meditates in the presence of the sovereignty of God.

If any man, woman, or child chooses to do the divine will, they shall know the way of the truth. It is literally true, "Human things must be known in order to be loved, but divine things must be loved in order to be known."

Though reason will always question faith, faith will always supersede both reason and logic. Reason creates the probability which faith can transform into a moral certainty, even a spiritual experience. God is the first truth and the last truth; therefore, does all truth take its origin from God.

God is absolute truth. As the truth, one may know God, but to understand, to explicate God, one must explore the fact through a child's eye. A child has faith in his parents who will come to his/her aid and protect him/her from the unknown. This same perception applies to the vast gulf between the experience of the truth of God, and ignorance as to the fact of God can be abridged only by living faith.

Belief may not be able to resist doubt and withstand fear, but faith is always triumphant over doubting, for faith is both positive and living. The positive always has the advantage over the negative, truth over error, experience over theory, spiritual realities over the isolated facts of time and space.

Man cannot enter into the Kingdom of heaven unless one is "born again," meaning born of the spirit. Man must realize that one's highest moral ideals are not necessarily synonymous with the will of God.

Man cannot hope to live up to his highest ideals, but he can be true to his purpose of finding God and becoming more and more like Him. God deals with His children on the basis, not of actual virtue or worthiness, but in recognition of the child's motivation, the creature purpose and intent. The relationship is one of parent-child association and is actuated by divine love.

The essence of religion is a progressive willingness to believe these assumptions of reason, wisdom, and faith. Religion must be motivated by truth and dominated by love.

Through truth, man attains beauty and by spiritual love ascends to goodness. True religion is thus an experience of believing and knowing as well as a satisfaction of feeling.

THE TRUTH ABOUT PRAYER

Prayer is a personal and spontaneous attitude of the soul, reaching toward the spirit. Prayer is the communion of Son to Father and the expression of fellowship. Prayer, when ignited by the spirit, leads to cooperative spiritual progress. The ideal prayer is a form of spiritual communion which leads to intelligent worship. True prayer is indicted with a sincere attitude in your attempt to ascertain the Father's will.

"Again, I say to you, ask and it shall be given you, seek and you shall find; knock and it shall be opened to you. For everyone who asks shall receive; he who seeks finds; and to him who knocks the door of salvation will be opened" (Matt. 7:7).

Men, women, and children ought to pray and not become discouraged. I encourage you to persist in praying. Your persistence, however, is not to win favor with God, but to change your spiritual progress.

Jesus taught to always pray in secret; to go off by yourselves amidst the quiet surroundings of your environment or to go to your private rooms and shut the doors when you engage in prayer. Jesus taught that effective prayer must be:

Unselfish—not alone for oneself.
Believing—according to faith.
Sincere—honest of heart.
Intelligent—according to light.
Trustful—in submission to the Father's all-wise will.

In praying, remember the relationship of Father to Son is a gift. The child of God comes into grace and the new life of the spirit by the will of the Father in Heaven.

Prayer, therefore, is the sincere and longing look of the child to its spirit of the Father; it is a psychological process of exchanging the human will for the divine will. Prayer is essentially a part of the divine plan for making over that which is into that which ought to be.

When you obtain the realization that you are saved by faith (i.e., when I was found not guilty of robbery in the first degree), you have real peace with God. All who follow in the way of this heavenly peace are destined to be sanctified to the eternal service of the everlasting sons of the Eternal God. Henceforth, it is not a duty but rather a privilege to cleanse yourselves from all evils in mind and body while you seek perfection in the love of God. The conscious and persistent regard for iniquity in the heart of man gradually destroys the prayer connection of the human soul to the Maker. Naturally, God hears the petition of His child, but when the human heart persistently and deliberately harbors the concepts of iniquity, there gradually ensues the loss of personal communication between earth child and the Heavenly Father.

He who rules his own self is greater than he who captures a city. Self-mastery is the measure of man's moral nature and the indicator of his spiritual development.

We need to believe and rejoice in the rebirth of the spirit.

By our love for one another we are to convince the world that we have successfully passed from bondage to liberty, from death into life everlasting.

Thus, by our faith and the spirit bestowed within each one of us, we become in reality the temples of God, his spirit actually dwells within us. If then the spirit dwells within you, you are no longer bondslaves of the flesh but free and liberated sons of the spirit. The human heart is deceitful above all things and sometimes even desperately wicked. It is easy to become self-deceived and thereby fall into, foolish fears, lust, enslaving pleasures (drugs), malice, envy, and even vengeful hatred.

Jesus quoted the proverb of the wise man who said, "He who turns away his ear from hearing the divine law even his prayer shall be an abomination."

When man hears God's spirit speak within the human heart, inherent in such an experience, is the fact that God simultaneously hears that prayer. Even the forgiveness of sin operates in this same unerring fashion. The Father in Heaven has forgiven you even before you have thought to ask Him, but such forgiveness is not available in your personal religious experience until such time as you forgive your fellow men. God's forgiveness, in fact, is not conditioned upon your fellows but in experience it is exactly so conditioned. This fact of the synchrony of divine and human forgiveness was thus recognized and linked together in the prayer which Jesus taught the apostles.

Jesus quoted from the Hebrew scriptures: "I have called and you refused to hear; I stretched out my hand, but no man regarded. You have set at naught all my counsel, and you have rejected my reproof and because of this rebellious attitude it becomes inevitable that you shall call upon me and fail to receive an answer. Having rejected the way of life, you may seek me diligently in your times of suffering, but you will not find me."

They who would receive mercy should show mercy, judge not that you be not judged. Mercy does not wholly abrogate universe fairness. With the spirit with which you judge others, you also will be judged. In the end, it will prove true: "Whosoever stops his ears to the cry of the poor, he also shall some day cry for help, and no one will hear him." The sincerity of any prayer is the assurance of its being heard, the spiritual wisdom and universe consistency of any petition is the determiner of the time, manner, and degree of the answer.

When we become wholly dedicated to the doing of the will of the Father in Heaven, the answer to all our petitions will be forthcoming because our prayers will be in full accordance with the Father's will, and the Father's will is ever manifest throughout His vast universe. What the true Son desires and infinite Father wills IS. Such a prayer cannot remain unanswered, and no other sort of petition can possibly be fully answered. The cry of the righteous is the faith act of the child of God which opens the door of the Father's storehouse of goodness, truth and mercy, and these good gifts have long been in awaiting for the Son's approach and personal appropriation. Prayer does not change the divine attitude toward man, but it does change mans attitude toward the changeless Father. The motive of the prayer gives it right away to the Divine ear, not the social, economic, or outward religious status of the one who prays.

Prayer is not designed as a technique for aggrandizing self or for gaining unfair advantage over one's fellows. A thoroughly selfish soul cannot pray in the true sense of the word. Said Jesus: "Let your supreme delight be in the character of God and He shall surely give you the sincere desires of your heart. Commit your way to the Lord; trust in Him, and He will act. For the Lord hears the cry of the needy, and He will regard the prayer of the destitute.

"I have come forth from the Father; therefore, you are ever in doubt as to what you would ask of the Father, ask in my name, and I will present your petition in accordance with your real needs and desires and in accordance with my Fathers will." Guard against the great danger of becoming self-centered in your prayers. Avoid praying much for yourself; pray more for the spiritual progress of your brothers and sisters. Avoid materialistic praying; pray in the spirit and for the abundance of gifts of the spirit.

When we pray for the sick and afflicted, do not expect that your petitions will take the place of loving and intelligent ministry to the necessities of these afflicted ones. Pray for the welfare of your families, friends, and fellows, but especially pray for those who curse you and make loving petitions for those who persecute you. But when to pray, I will not say. Only the spirit that dwells within you may move you to the utterance of these petitions which are expressive of your inner relationship with the Father of spirits.

Many people resort to prayer only when in trouble. Such a practice is thoughtless and misleading. True, you do well to pray when harassed, but you should also be mindful to speak as a son to your Father even when all goes well with your soul. Let your real petitions always be in secret. Do not let men hear your personal prayers. Prayers of thanksgiving are appropriate for groups of worshipers but the prayer of the soul is a personal matter. There is but one form of prayer which is appropriate for all God's children, and that is: "Nevertheless, your will be done."

All believers in the true gospel should pray sincerely for the extension of the Kingdom of Heaven. Of all the prayers of the Hebrew scriptures, he commented most approvingly on the petition of the Psalmist: "Create in me a clean heart, oh God, and renew a right spirit within me. Purge me from secret sins and keep back your servant from presumptuous transgression" (Ps. 51:10).

Jesus commented at great length on the relation of prayer to cureless and offending speech, Jesus said, "Set a watch, Oh Lord, before my mouth; keep the door of my lips. The human tongue," said Jesus, "is a member which few men can tame, but the spirit within can transform this unruly member into a kindly voice of tolerance and an inspiring minister of mercy."

Jesus taught that the prayer for divine guidance over the pathway of earthly life was next in importance to the petition for a knowledge of the Father's will. In reality, this means a prayer for divine wisdom. Jesus never taught that human knowledge and special skill could be gained by prayer. He did teach that prayer is a factor in the enlargement of one's capacity to receive the presence of the divine spirit. When Jesus taught his associates to pray in the Spirit and in truth, He explained that He referred to praying sincerely and in accordance with one's enlightenment to praying wholeheartedly and intelligently, earnestly and steadfastly.

It is written that Jesus warned his followers against that their prayers would be rendered more efficacious by ornate receptions, eloquent phraseology, fasting or sacrifices. But He did exhort His believers to employ prayer as a means of leading up through thanksgiving to true worship. Jesus deplored that so little of the spirit of thanksgiving was to be found in the prayers and worship of His followers. He quoted from the scriptures on this occasion, saying, "It is a good thing to give thanks to the Lord and to sing praises to the name of the Most High, to acknowledge his loving kindness every morning and his faithfulness every night, for God has made me glad through His work. In everything I will give thanks according to the will of God."

Then Jesus said: "Be not constantly overanxious about your common needs. Be not apprehensive concerning the problems of your earthly existence, but in all these things by prayer and supplication, with the spirit of sincere thanksgiving let your needs be spread out before your Father who is in Heaven." Then he quoted from the scriptures: "I will praise the name of God with a song and will magnify him with thanksgiving. And this will please the Lord better than the sacrifice of an ox or bullock with horns and hooves."

Jesus taught his followers that, when they had made their prayers to the Father, they should remain for a time in silent receptivity to afford the indwelling spirit the better opportunity to speak to the listening soul. The spirit of the Father speaks best to man when the human mind is an attitude of true worship.

We worship God by the aid of the Father's indwelling spirit and by the illumination of the human mind through the ministry of truth. Worship, taught Jesus, makes one increasingly like the being who is worshiped. Worship is a transforming experience whereby the Finite gradually approaches and ultimately attains the presence of the Infinite.

THE EVOLUTION OF PRAYER

Prayer, unless in liaison with the will and actions of the personal spiritual forces and material supervisors of a realm, can have no direct effect upon one's physical environment.

While there is a very definite limit to the province of the petitions of prayer, such limits do not equally apply to the faith of those who actually pray.

Prayer is not a technique for curing real and organic diseases, but it has contributed enormously to the enjoyment of abundant health and to the run of numerous mental, emotional, and nervous ailments. Even in actual bacterial disease, prayer has many times added to the efficacy of other remedial procedures. Prayer has turned many an irritable and complaining invalid into a paragon of patience and made him an inspiration to all other human sufferers.

No matter how difficult it may be to reconcile the scientific doubting regarding the efficacy of prayer with the ever-present urge to seek help and guidance from divine sources, never forget that the sincere prayer of faith is a mighty force for the promotion of personal happiness, individual self-control, social harmony, moral progress, and spiritual attainment.

Prayer, even as a purely human practice, a dialogue with one's alter ego, constitutes a technique of the most efficient approach to the realization of those reserve powers of human nature which are stored and conserved in the unconscious realms of the human mind. Prayer is a sound psychological practice, aside from its religious implications and its spiritual significance. It is a fact of human experience that most persons, if sufficiently hard pressed, will pray in some way to some source of help.

Do not be slothful as to ask God to solve your difficulties, but never hesitate to ask Him for wisdom and spiritual strength to guide and sustain you while you yourself resolutely and courageously attack the problem at hand.

Prayer has been an indispensable factor in the progress and preservation of religious civilization, and it still has mighty contributions to make to the further enhancement and spiritualization of society if those who pray will only do so in the light of scientific bets, philosophic wisdom, intellectual sincerity, and spiritual faith. Pray as Jesus taught his disciples, honestly, unselfishly, with fairness, and without doubting.

Prayer may become an established custom; many pray because others do. Still others pray because they fear something dire may happen if they do not offer their regular supplications.

To some people, individual prayer is the calm expression of gratitude; to others, a group expression of praise, social devotions; while in true praying, it is the sincere and trusting communication of the spiritual nature of the creature with the anywhere presence of the spirit of the Creator.

Prayer may be a spontaneous expression of God's consciousness or a meaningless recitation of theological formulas. It may be the ecstatic praise of a God-knowing soul or the slavish obeisance of a fear ridden human. It is sometimes the pathetic expression of spiritual craving and sometimes the blatant shouting of pious phrases. Prayer may be a joyous praise or a humble plea for forgiveness.

Prayer may be the childlike plea for the impossible or the mature entreaty for moral growth and spiritual power. A petition may be for daily bread or may embody a wholehearted yearning to find God and to do His will. It may be a wholly selfish request or a true and magnificent gesture toward the realization of unselfish brotherhood.

Prayer may be an angry cry for vengeance or an intercession for one's enemies. It may be the expression of a hope of changing God or the powerful technique of changing one's self. It may be the cringing plea of a lost sinner before a supposedly stern judge or the joyful expression of a liberated son of the living and merciful Heavenly Father.

Humans are perplexed by he thought of talking things over with God in a purely personal way. Many have abandoned regular praying; they only pray when under unusual pressure in emergencies. Man should be unafraid to talk to God but only a spiritual child would undertake to persuade or presume to change God.

But real praying does attain reality. Even when the air currents are ascending, no bird can soar except by outstretched wings. Prayer elevates man because it is a technique of progressing by the utilization of the ascend ing *spiritual* currents of the universe.

Genuine prayer adds to spiritual growth, modifies attitudes, and yields that satisfaction which comes from communion with divinity. It is a spontaneous outburst of God-consciousness. God answers man's prayer by giving him an increased revelation of truth, an enhanced appreciation of beauty, and an augmented concept of goodness. Prayer is a subjective gesture, but it contacts with mighty objective realities on the spiritual levels of human experience, it is meaningful reach by the human for superhuman values. It is the most potent spiritual-growth stimulus.

Words, therefore, are irrelevant to prayer; they are merely the intellectual channel in which the river of spiritual supplication may have a chance to flow. The word value of a prayer is purely auto-suggestive in private devotions and socio-suggestive in group devotions. God answers the soul attitude, not the words.

Prayer is not a technique of escape from conflict but rather a stimulus to growth in the very face of conflict. So therefore, pray only for *values*, not *things*, for *growth*, not for *gratification*.

CONDITIONS OF EFFECTIVE PRAYER

If men, women, and children engage in effective prayer, one should bear in mind the laws of prevailing petitions:

— You must qualify as a potent prayer by sincerely and courageously facing the problems of universal reality. Belief and trusting stamina is a must.

— You must have honestly exhausted the human capacity for human adjustment. You must have been industrious.

— You must surrender every wish of mind and every craving of soul to the transforming embrace of spiritual growth. You must have experienced an enhancement of meanings and elevation of values.

— You must make a wholehearted choice of the divine will. You must obliterate the dead center of indecision.

— You must not only recognize the Father's will and choose to do it, but you have effected an unqualified consecration, and the dynamic dedication to the actual doing of the Father's will.

— Your prayer must be directed exclusively for the divine wisdom to solve specific human problems.

— You must have faith (living faith).

THE TRUTH ABOUT SIN

Human sin is the attitude of a personality who is knowingly resisting truth and acceptance of God.

Evil is a partial realization of or maladjustment to universal realities. But sin is a purposeful resistance to divine reality (a conscious choosing to oppose spiritual progress), while iniquity consists of an open and persistent defiance of recognized reality and signifies such a degree of personality disintegration as to border on cosmic insanity.

Error suggests lack of intellectual keenness, evil, deficiency of wisdom, sin, abject poverty; but iniquity is indicative of vanishing personality control.

When sin has so many times been chosen and so often been repeated, it may become habitual. Habitual sinners can easily become iniquitous, rebels against the universe and all of its divine realities. While all manner of sins may be forgiven, we doubt whether the established iniquiter would ever or will ever sincerely experience sorrow for his misdeeds or accept forgiveness for his sins

Sin, being the attitude of the person toward reality, is destined to exhibit its inherent negative harvest upon any and all related levels of universe values. But the full consequences of erroneous thinking, evil-doing, or sinful planning are experienced only on the level of actual performers. Sin is fraught with fatal consequences to personality survival only when it is the attitude of the whole being, when it stands for choosing of the mind and the willing of the soul.

Evil and sin visit their consequences in material and social realms and may sometimes even retard certain levels of universal reality, but never does the sin of any being rob another of the realization of the divine right of personality survival. Eternal survival can be jeopardized by the decisions of the mind and the soul of the individual himself.

Sin enormously retards intellectual development, moral growth, social progress, and mass spiritual attainment. But it does not prevent the highest spiritual achievement by any individual who chooses to know God and sincerely do His divine will.

No person is ever made to suffer vital spiritual deprivation because of the sin of another. Sin is wholly personal as to moral guilt or spiritual consequences, notwithstanding its far-flung repercussions in administrative, intellectual, and social domains.

Sin must be redefined as deliberate disloyalty to Deity. There are degrees of disloyalty Deity; the partial loyalty of indecision, the divided loyalty of confliction, the dying loyalty of indifference, and the death of loyalty exhibited in devotion to Godless ideals.

The sense or feeling of guilt is the consciousness of the violation of the mores, it is not necessarily sin. There is no real sin in the absence of conscious disloyalty to Deity.

The possibility of the recognition of the sense of guilt is a badge of transcendent distinction for mankind. It does not mark man as mean but rather sets him apart as a creature of potential greatness and ever-ascending glory. Such a sense of unworthiness is the initial stimulus that should lend quickly and surely to those faith conquests which translate the mortal mind to the superb levels of moral nobility, cosmic insight, and spiritual living, thus are all values and meanings of human existence changed from the temporal to the eternal, and all values are elevated from the human to the divine.

The confession of sin is a manful repulciation of disloyalty, but in no way mitigates the time-space consequences of such disloyalty. Confession—sincere recognition of the nature of sin—is essential to religious growth and spiritual progress

THE TRUTH ABOUT MAGIC
AND SUPERSTITION

Astronomy is a proper pursuit of science, but astrology is the *mass* of superstitious error which has no place in the gospel of the kingdom.

The spirits of the dead do not come back to communicate with their families or their one-time friends among the living.

Charms and relics are important to heal disease, ward off disaster, or influence evil spirits; however, the belief in all such material means of influencing the spiritual world is nothing but gross superstition.

The only means of communion with the spiritual world is embraced in the spirit endowment of mankind, the indwelling spirit of the Father, together with the outpoured spirit of the Son and Omnipresent influence of the Infinite Spirit (God).

Sorcery and witchcraft are superstitions of ignorant minds, as also are delusions of magic. The belief in magic numbers, omens of good luck, and harbingers of bad luck, is pure and unfounded superstition.

The interpretation of dreams, for the most part, is a biased, opinionated, diagnostic, superstitious, and groundless system of ignorant and fanatic speculation.

The spirits of good or evil cannot dwell within material symbols of clay, wood, or metal; idols are nothing more than the material of which they are made from.

Jesus exposed and denounced human belief in spells, ordeals, bewitching, cursing, signs, mandrakes, knotted cords, and all other forms of ignorant and enslaving superstition.

GUIDELINES FOR SPIRITUAL LIBERATION

All religions are good to the extent that they bring man to God and bring the realization of the Father to man.

True religion is a way of living as well as a technique of teaching and thinking.

The religious experience of children is largely dependent on whether fear or love has dominated the parent-child relationship. Religious meanings progress in self-consciousness when the child transfers his ideas of omnipotence from his parents to God.

In union there is strength and it is this lack of natural brotherly attraction that now stands in the way of immediate realization of the brotherhood of man on Earth.

Groups are vastly greater and stronger than the mere sum of their individual units; therefore, the church is more powerful than the church member by himself.

The evolution of a religious-based social philosophy affords its peoples a contrastive illustration of the function of the church as an institution in the shaping and preservation of cultural progress.

Judge not, that you be not judged.

Happy are those who are persecuted for righteousness sake, for theirs is the Kingdom of Heaven.

When you know that you are saved by faith, you have real peace with God.

He who rules his own self is greater than the judge who sits on the bench and administers injustice against the poor, the humble, and the meek.

In the time of testing, a man's soul is revealed; trial and tribulation discloses what really is in the heart.

If you presume to exalt yourselves before God you will certainly be humbled; but whosoever truly humbles himself will surely be exalted. Seek in your daily lives no self-glorification, but the glory of God. Intelligently subordinate your own wills to the will of the Father in Heaven.

Of those who listen to the truth and believe it superficially with their minds, few of them permit the word of truth to strike down into the heart with thriving roots. "Jah, rastafari man." Thank you, Bob Marley.

Those who know the gospel only in the mind and who have not experienced it in the heart cannot be depended upon for support when real trouble comes.

The love call of the spiritual kingdom should prove to be the effective destroyer of the hate urge of the unbelieving and war-minded citizens of the earthly kingdoms.

As mortal and material men we are indeed citizens of the earthly kingdoms and we should be good citizens. All the better for having become reborn spirit sons of the Heavenly Kingdom. As faith-enlightened as spirit liberated sons of the kingdom of Heaven, we face a double responsibility of duty to man and duty to God while we voluntarily assume a third and sacred obligation: Service to the brotherhood of God-knowing believers.

We should manifest the righteous ministry of loving service to believers and unbelievers alike. In the gospel of the Kingdom there resides the mighty Spirit of Truth, and presently the Father will pour out this same spirit upon all flesh. The fruit of the spirit, your sincere and loving service, are the mighty social lever to uplift the races of prejudice (*racism*), and this Spirit of Truth will become our power-multiplying fulcrum.

Display wisdom and exhibit sagacity (shrewdness) in your dealings with unbelieving civil rulers and common folk. By discretion, show yourselves to be expert in ironing out minor and major disagreements. Seek to live peaceably with all men.

The attitude of unselfish service man and intelligent worship of God should make all Kingdom believers better world citizens. As long as rulers of earthly government seek to exercise the authority of materialistic dictators, you who believe this gospel can expect only trouble, you bear to the world, and even the very manner in which you will suffer and die for this gospel of the Kingdom will, in themselves, eventually enlighten the whole world and result in the gradual development of politics and religion.

The persistent preaching of the gospel of the Kingdom will some day bring to all nations a new and unbelievable liberation, intellectual freedom and religious liberty.

Learn to be faithful, steadfast revolutionaries for the Kingdom even in times of peace and prosperity. Tempt not the needs of the devil's demons to lead you in troubling ways as a loving comrade designed to save your east-drifting souls.

You must never allow anything to divert your devotion to this one duty: Love and let all mankind benefit from the overflow of your loving spiritual ministry, enlightening intellectual communion, and uplifting social service, but none of these humanitarian labors, nor all of them, should be permitted to take the place of proclaiming the gospel.

50

Every Minister a Strategist

Strategists will ask certain questions about their ministries such as:

Who is my target for ministry?
Where are they located?
What are their felt needs?
How do I establish contact?
How can that contact lead to a sharing of the Gospel?
If they respond to the Gospel, how can they be enfolded into a healthy Christian community?

Some Do s for an Effective Ministry:

— Do your ministry as a result of your relationship with the Lord rather than to try to earn His favor.

— Do pray for and seek like-minded people to get involved with you; Lone Ranger ministries often become casualties.

— Do specialize; learn the art of "This one thing I do," rather than "These forty things I dabble at."

— Do discern your area of spiritual giftedness and work in the areas of your strengths; it is very difficult to stay motivated working in your areas of weakness.

— Do learn to say "No" to things that are good but will sidetrack you from the best.

— Do commit yourself to being a lifetime student. In general, pursue the basic spiritual disciplines; and in particular, you read, study, and become a resource person in your special area of ministry.

— Do try to work out your ministry as a recognized part of your local church's ministry and remain accountable to the church's leadership.

— Do you, for inner motivation, ask God what He wants you to do? Do realize that all ministries have highs and lows. When our Lord calls you to a ministry, He does not promise you a rose garden.

Some Don ts for an Effective Ministry:

— Don't fall into the trap of loving your ministry more than your Lord.

— Don't lay guilt trips on others for not getting involved in your ministry. Allow God to work in people, and until He does, assume the timing is not right.

— Don't let failures stop you; unless God makes it very clear He has shut the door, keep on trying.

— Don't neglect signs of burn-out; don't allow yourself to continue out of guilt motivation or out of a desire to please someone other than the Lord.

— Don't be afraid to quit when you have peace from the Lord that it is time to do so.

— Don't fall into the trap of "Our ministry is more special than other ministries." It is a trap that tends to create first and second class citizens in the church, and in Christ's Body there are no second class citizens.

Importance of Setting Priorities:

Are you keeping up in your devotional life and prayer time?
Are you spending quality time with your family?
Are you sharing your faith with non-Christians?
Are you studying and memorizing scripture?
Are you helping younger and newer Christians grow in their faith?

Only if we set our priorities and realize the significance of what we are doing for God's greater glory, can we keep on keeping on. We can then stay on course.

Success is up to God; our responsibility is just to be obedient.

A sense of duty is not enough for long-haul motivation, a sense of purpose is.

God works when we pray—first things first, realize the power of prayer. "O Lord, God of Heaven, the great and awesome God."

Your Special Call to Ministry:

To be effective witnesses, servants, and disciples in our Christian lives, every believer must make certain basic, personal commitments to:

A daily devotional time.
The study of God's word.
A consistent and serious prayer life.
A personal commitment to the great commission.
A life-style that is totally pleasing to God.

We must be committed to these basics if we intend to be serious about ministry.

Final Thoughts

It must be borne in mind that the tragedy in life doesn't lie in not reaching your goal. The tragedy lies in having no goal to reach.

"It isn't a calamity to die with dreams unfulfilled, but it is a calamity not to dream. It is not a disaster to be unable to capture your ideal, but it is a disaster to have no ideal to capture. It is not a disgrace not to reach for the stars, but it is a disgrace to have no stars to reach for. Not failure, but low aim is sin.

"It will not be sufficient for Morehouse College, for any college for that matter, to produce clever graduates, men fluent in speech and able to argue their way through; but rather honest men, men who can be trusted in public and private who are sensitive to wrongs, and injustices of society and who are willing to accept responsibility for correcting the ills."

—*Benjamin E. Mays*

The bad boy, indeed, I am you. Not just pieces which you pick and choose, but the whole of you, good and the bad. Since I am you, why not accept me?

My truth in me will reach for the truth in you. So, sow the seeds of wisdom and truth and continue to share the gospel.

Divine Love,
Adisa

The Brotherhood of the Brave New World Order

Ethical Standards and Bylaws

The B.B.N.W.O. is comprised of professional persons who, as responsible citizens, believe in the dignity and worth of all human beings. In practice of their professions, they assert the ethical principals of authority, beneficence, and justice should guide their daily conduct. As religious people dedicated to the fair treatment of all Americans and other American minorities here in America and abroad, our family manifests. The B.B.N.W.O. dedicates themselves to promote the best interests of themselves and their society.

Specific Principles

Principle 1: Non-Violence

The B.B.N.W.O. will not use or associate any use of violence against any group of people who don't belong or oppose the B.B.N.W.O. Violence only becomes acceptable when it is used to Defend oneself against the perpetrators of genocide. Violence may also be used to protect one's family from physical aggression or attacks from individuals or group activities that are associated with hate philosophies.

Principle 2: Non-Discrimination

The B.B.N.W.O. should not discriminate against other people's religion, age, handicaps, offender status, national ancestry, sexual orientation, or economic conditions.

Principle 3: Communal Standards and Moral Codes

The B.B.N.W.O. should uphold the accepted moral codes that pertain to professional conduct and daily living. The B.B.N.W.O. should not use the brotherhood for the purposes not consistent with the stated purpose of the brotherhood. The B.B.N.W.O. should not associate with or permit the organization's name to be used in connection with any services or products in a way that is incorrect or misleading. The brotherhood member's and colleagues associated with the development or the promotion of the literature or other products for commercial sales should be responsible for ensuring that such literature products are presented in a professional way. The B.B.N.W.O. will uphold the legal requirements for confidentiality of all records, materials, and communications regarding members and their families, and respect for the rights and views of colleagues and members shall be demonstrated. Any member who is aware of unethical conduct shall be demonstrated. Any member who is aware of unethical conduct or detrimental or unprofessional modes of behavior should report any such violations to the appropriate certifying authority. Any member who shows professional impairment on professional performance must be willing to seek appropriate treatment or risk termination of membership.

Principle 4: Public Statements

The B.B.N.W.O. members who represent the organization of other agencies, organizations, and perspective members should respect the limits of present knowledge in public statements concerning the order. The B.B.N.W.O. should fairly and accurately appropriate information to the media. Members must document materials and techniques used in deploying information to the media.

Principle 5: Membership Welfare

The B.B.N.W.O. should respect the integrity and protect the welfare of the members and their families. The brotherhood should set up a defense fund to aid in the area of bail monies, lawyer fees, and court costs. This fund will be held in escrow and used solely for the purpose of litigation and personal tragedy or emergencies and special tributes. The B.B.N.W.O. should define for self and others the nature and direction of loyalties and responsibilities and keep all parties concerned informed of these decisions and commitments. As members of the B.B.N.W.O., we must be supremely vigilant to not stand judgment or make assumptions about other values and beliefs of those belonging to them, such as their name or family background.

Principle 6: Secrecy

The B.B.N.W.O. is protected by a collective vow of secrecy. No member is to disclose any information to any outsider without the expressed permission from the board of directors.

Principle 7: Lifetime Membership

Each member of the B.B.N.W.O. is a lifetime member and is protected and serviced under the code of ethical standards and bylaws of the B.B.N.W.O. Resignation will be accepted in writing and upon review of the board of directors. Initial membership fees are $25 and are $15 each year thereafter.

If you are interested in establishing a chapter of "The Brotherhood of the Brave New World Order," you can obtain a free copy of the constitution, ethical standards and bylaws by sending an email of interest to:

bhood1@highland.net

Founder: Adisa Breckinridge-Ayers

REFERENCES

King, Reverend Martin Luther, Jr. Distributed by the Martin Luther King, Jr. Center for Social Change. Atlanta, Georgia.

Forrest, Gary G. Ed, D, Ph.D. *Chemical Dependency and Anti-Social Personality Disorders: Psychotherapy and Assessment Strategies.* Haworth Press, Inc., 1994, p43, p56.

Center for Disease Control; Reports 1993-1994. United States, Atlanta, Georgia.

Associated Press, Oakland Tribune, unknown author, January, 1995.

Sentencing Project, Reports 1993-1994, Honolulu Advertiser, Associated Press, September 13, 1994.

Edelman, Wright Marian. President of the Children's Defense Fund (personal quote).

Reibstein, Larry, Back to the Chain Gang?" *Newsweek* (October 17, 1994): pg 87-90.

McCormick, John, "Death of a Child Criminal,) *Newsweek* (October 17, 1994):

Time. "Murder in Miniature" by Richard Lacayo, September 19, 1994 p 60-63.

Breckenridge, Tyrone. "Apathetic Personality Disorder", December 1993.

"National Center for Health Statistics", Reports 1993-1994, United States.

Constitution, "Excerpt" United States.

Associated Press, Oakland Tribune, unknown author, January, 1995.

Payton, Brenda, eds. (Oakland Tribune) January 17-19, 1995.

Time. "Murder in Miniature" by Nancy R. Gibbs, September 19, 1994

Ebony, South Africa's New Leadership. Johnson and Johnson Publishing Col, Vol. SLIX, No. 10, p. 104-108. Quote by: Dr. Cheika Anta Diop, August 1994.

Malcolm X, "By Any Means Necessary" (personal quote).

"Sentencing Project", Reports 1993-1994. Honolulu Advertiser, Associated Press. September 13, 1994.

Ebony, "South Africa's New Leadership", Johnson and Johnson Publishing Co., Vol. XLIX, No. 10, p. 104-108. Quote by: Richard Hatcher, August 1994.

F.A.M.M. (Families Against Mandatory Minimums). FAMM Foundation, Washington, D.C.

Urantia Foundation. Chicago, IL: 1955. *The Urantia Book,* p. 984, 999 1001,1002, 1083, 1086, 1087, 1088, 1089, 1091, 1092, 1093, 1118, 1125, 1130, 1133, 1141, 1142, 1429, 1618, 1619, 1620, 1621, 1638, 1639, 1640, 1641, 1680, 1681.